ONTARIO COUNTRY DIARY

ONTARIO COUNTRY DIARY

Susan Perry and Joe McKendy

A Centennial College Press
Publication,
produced exclusively for

NELSON/CANADA

Nelson Canada Limited
81 Curlew Drive, Don Mills, Ontario
M3A 2R1

Cover Design: Paul Weldon, Design Collaborative

Photographs courtesy of Ontario Ministry of
Industry and Tourism

Photographs on pages 27, 33, 44, 48, 59, 87, 92,
and 124 by Susan Perry

Typesetting: Teresa Belliveau

Printed and bound in Canada
123456 WC 76543210

ISBN 0-17-601415-2

Introduction

Rural Ontario has a lot to offer. And Ontario Country Diary will lead you to many of its most exciting places and activities.

The Fairs

This section of Ontario Country Diary is a comprehensive guide to over 600 fairs, festivals, carnivals, and other celebrations. Each listing consists of a brief description of the event, its location, and the date or dates when it is usually held. Many listings include a phone number to call for date and time confirmation. Where phone numbers are not included, a call to the nearest Ontario Travel Information Centre is recommended. These Centres are listed on page 127.

The Towns

This section of Ontario Country Diary lists over 125 towns and describes their antique shops, flea markets, wildlife sanctuaries, pick-your-own farms, country stores, restaurants, and other local attractions.

Ontario Country Diary is a book to be used as well as read. The fairs are listed by season, then by approximate date, the towns, alphabetically. Here's a suggestion for getting the most out of the book. Pick a fair you'd like to visit and check its location on the appropriate map, using the index on p.125. When you've located it on a map, take note of the other towns in the vicinity and look in The Towns section to see what they have to offer. Chances are you'll be able to combine a visit to a fair with taking in some local attractions.

Ontario Country Diary is a comprehensive guide to rural Ontario that will provide you with the information you need to enjoy the country. And while it would be impossible to list everything the country has to offer, the book includes a sampling of so many activities and places, there's sure to be something for every interest.

The
Fairs

Travel notes

Winter

This winter, instead of complaining about the ice and snow, why not slide on it, skate on it, and play in it? Across Ontario, carnivals and festivals celebrate this chilly winter season.

Most of these winter events include snow sculpture contests, dogsled races, ice-fishing derbys, and snowmobile, snowshoeing, and cross-country skiing races. Others feature the unusual and daring — zany bed races, polar bear dips, motorcycle races on ice, and a snowsnake tournament.

Many carnivals offer refreshments from outdoor soup kettles, barbecues, and bonfires. And there's always plenty of hot chocolate.

Some of the activities are spectator oriented, but many encourage participation. Take along ice skates, toboggans, and skis; dress warmly, and join in the fun.

Annual Christmas Parade

Blenheim

Plan to bring the children to this old-fashioned, small town parade, and capture the Christmas spirit.

usually held the first Saturday in December

Annual Sale of Arts and Crafts

Guelph — (519) 822-1260

The Willow West Mall is the place to find some unique gifts.

usually held the first Sunday in December

Christmas Parade

Niagara-on-the-Lake — (416) 468-2322

Yes, Virginia, there is a Santa Claus. And he's in this old-fashioned parade that both young and old will enjoy.

usually held the second Saturday in December

Christmas Festival Days

Fergus — (519) 846-5169

Find the true Christmas spirit through displays, sleigh rides and refreshments at the Wellington County Museum. No Scrooges, please!

usually held the second and third Sundays in December

Christmas at the Thomas House

Oakville — (416) 845-3952

All ages will enjoy this re-creation of an 1850 Christmas on the farm, complete with decorating and baking.

usually held the third weekend in December

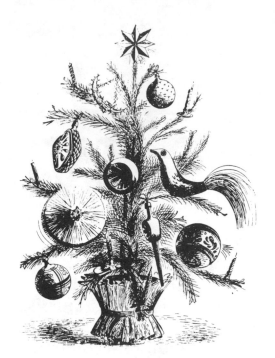

Christmas cheer

Combine two of Ontario's best known products — maple syrup and apple cider — to make this unique wine.

Cider-Maple Wine

You'll need 3 quarts of fresh apple cider, one pint of pure maple syrup, baker's or wine yeast, and a large crock. Heat the syrup and combine it with the cider in the crock. Mix well. Sprinkle the yeast on top and cover with a heavy towel. Place in a warm spot and stir every day for two weeks. Strain into a fermentation jar (a glass jar with a fermentation lock, available at wine making stores) and let it do its magic in a cool spot. Bottle when the wine is clear and still.

If you start in the fall, the wine will be ready for serving on Christmas Eve.

Victorian Christmas

Kitchener

Discover the joys of Christmas' past, at the Woodside National Historic Park.

usually held the last two weeks in December

Christmas Torchlight Parade

Huntsville

Watch the spectacular beauty of skiers winding their way down the mountain with lit torches.

usually takes place on Christmas Eve

O Christmas tree

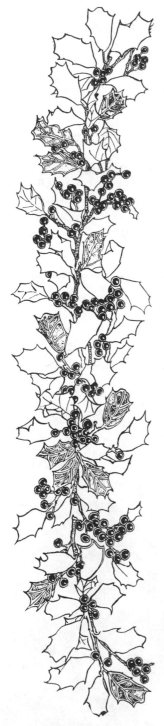
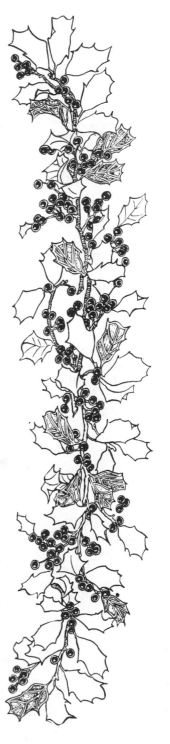

When you're dreaming of a white Christmas, the only welcome bit of green is the Christmas tree.

Trees have had symbolic meanings for thousands of years. Ancient Egyptians, Chinese, and Hebrews identified wreaths of evergreen boughs with eternal life. The Romans also regarded trees as a positive symbol; they marked each new year by exchanging green tree branches for good luck.

Our modern tradition of the Christmas tree is firmly rooted in Germany. And there are several stories that explain how the tradition emerged.

The most famous story of the Christmas tree is that of St. Bonafice of Crediton, an English missionary in 8th century Germany. It is said that one Christmas Eve, he came upon an oak tree, under which a human sacrifice had been offered during a pagan ritual. St. Bonafice chopped down the oak and immediately, a young fir tree appeared in its place. From then on, the fir tree was known as a symbol of Christianity and was displayed at Christmas.

One German legend tells that even though it was the middle of winter, trees bloomed and bore fruit on the night Christ was born. As a result of this legend, people brought cherry, pear, or hawthorne boughs indoors in winter and put them in water so they'd bloom during the Christmas season.

Some people say that the Christmas tree's present status evolved from its use in a medieval play concerning the story of Adam and Eve. The set was furnished with a fir tree with apples hanging from it. Consequently, it became customary to set up a tree in the home on December 24, to commemorate the feast day of Adam and Eve. Another custom of the time was to set up shelves in the home with Christmas figurines, evergreen boughs, candles, and other Christmas items. Eventually, these decorative articles came to be hung on the tree.

Another belief concerning the decoration of Christmas trees is that Martin Luther originated the practice. One story says that he was out walking one Christmas Eve and was so moved by the beauty of the evergreen trees and stars that he brought a tree indoors and attached candles to its branches in an effort to recreate that beauty.

Christmas trees were common among German Lutherans during the 17th and 18th centuries. By the early 1800s, the custom had spread to England. It became very popular in England during the time of Queen Victoria, since her family included a tree as a focal point in their Christmas celebrations. Soon, the trees were popular in many Christian cultures.

Winter Carnival

Jordan — (416) 562-5726

Ball's Falls Conservation Area is the site of Jordan's winter carnival which includes snowmobile rides and races, hay rides, ice skating, motorcycle and auto races on the ice, outdoor soup kettles and a bake sale.

usually held in mid-January

Winterfest

Kitchener — (519) 578-2969

The many winter activities at this festival are highlighted by a snowmobile race.

usually held in mid-January

Winter Carnival

Owen Sound

Owen Sound hosts a week-long winter carnival of fun family activities. Spectator and participant activities include snowmobile races, dogsled races, parades, pancake breakfasts, sporting events and many other winter carnival treats.

usually held the second weekend through the third weekend in January

Winter Festival

Niagara Falls

Enjoy the festival spirit amidst the beauty of the Falls in winter. Events include an arts & crafts show and sale, a dance, a broomball tournament, special museum displays, plus other winter activities.

two weeks long, this festival is usually held the third and fourth weeks of January

Sno Sports Festival

Wyoming — (519) 845-3387

With physical fitness in mind (and fun too!), Wyoming celebrates winter. Family activities include a parade, snowmobile races, cross-country skiing, food booths, and displays.

usually held the third weekend in January

Winter Carnival

Minden

Minden's carnival includes a parade, broomball tournament, sleigh rides, dances, snowmobile races, and believe it or not, auto racing on an oval track made of solid ice.

usually held the last weekend in January

Robbie Burns Festival

Fergus

Join in Fergus' salute to Scottish heritage and that famous Scottish poet/philosopher, Robbie Burns. Highland dancing and instruction, Scottish costumes, tours of the area, a pipes tattoo, and a special dinner and dance are featured.

usually held the last weekend in January

Winter Jamboree

Wasaga Beach

The highlight of this festival is the Classic Snowmobile Racing Competition. The festival also features ice skating, a dance, a torchlight parade, and a cookout.

usually held in late January

Six Nations Snowsnake Tournament

Brantford — (519) 759-2650

What's a Snowsnake Tournament? Come to Brantford and find out. Entrants from across Canada and the U.S. will be competing. There are also Indian arts and crafts, and refreshments.

usually held late January or early February

Other communities holding **Winter Carnivals** in January include: Peterborough — second week; Seaforth — third weekend; Pembroke — last week; and Madoc — the last weekend in January.

Mulled Wine

Here's something to warm you and lift your spirits on a cold, snowy winter's eve.
1/2 cup each of raisins, slivered or whole almonds,
and sugar
zest of 1 orange
1/4 cup brandy
cardamon, cinnamon sticks, cloves, and nutmeg, to taste
1 litre red wine
Soak the raisins, almonds, orange zest, spices, and sugar in the brandy for a few hours.

Heat the mixture with the red wine slowly until steaming. Serve the wine in mugs with a cinnamon stick.

Snowsnakes

Snowsnakes are probably the fastest and longest snakes in Ontario. But there's no need to fear them.

A snowsnake is a long, waxed wooden shaft that is used in an annual Iroquois sporting event held each winter in Brantford. Competitors throw these shafts of wood like spears through long, narrow troughs in the snow, attempting to get the maximum distance from their throw.

Distances are marked as players on a team throw in succession. Whoever throws furthest gets a point for his team. It takes 4 points to win a game and if after 4 throws, a competitor's snakes have placed first each time, it's called a "game out." There is no limit to how many teams can play so it could take a long time for a team to achieve 4 throws of the longest distance. A team often has one thrower with 4 snowsnakes or 2 throwers with 2 snowsnakes each.

Players may take a running start when throwing and they may throw underhand or overhand. Timing, strength, dexterity, and the snake itself are crucial to how far the snake will travel. The snake is made by a member of a team referred to as the shiner. He chooses a young hardwood tree from which he makes the shaft. The most important thing to be aware of when selecting a snowsnake is balance, a major consideration when choosing a snowsnake for particular weather conditions. The snowsnake is shaped, polished, and shellacked so that it will slide easily through the snow. Molten lead is applied to the tip of the snake to form an arrow-like head.

The track's starting point is a mound of snow 1 metre high that slopes gradually to the end of the run. The trough in the snow is made by dragging a log of about 4 or 6 inches in diameter back and forth.

The snowsnake tournament was one of the Iroquois' national games even before the white man came to North America. And just as the Indian game of lacrosse was the forerunner to the game of hockey, maybe the snowsnake was the inspiration for today's javelin throwing competitions.

Winter Weekend

Oakville — (416) 827-6911

Bronte Creek Provincial Park is the site of sleigh rides, snow sculpturing, snowshoeing, and cross-country skiing. Satisfy your hunger with homemade soup from the outdoor soup kettle.

usually held the first weekend in February

Ground Hog Festival

Wiarton

Will the ground hog see his shadow? Find out in this festival atmosphere. Snowmobile races, curling, and a beauty pageant are just some of the highlights.

usually held the first weekend in February

Winter Carnival

Grimsby — (416) 945-2208

This carnival is held around the Grimsby Village Depot, a railway station restored to its early 20th century appearance. Festivities include snow sculpturing, hay rides, outdoor soup kettles, and cider booths.

usually held in early February

Heritage Festival

Elora — (519) 846-9711

This picturesque town becomes even more beautiful during this mid-winter festival where heritage costumes are worn. Arts and crafts, snow sculpturing, square dancing, a log sawing contest, and a torchlight parade are all part of the festivities.

usually held the second Saturday in February

Winter Carnival

Stoney Point — (519) 798-3032

Snowmobile racing, ice racing, and an ice fishing derby are some of the features of this carnival.

usually held the second weekend in February

Winter Carnival

Barrie

Kempenfeldt Bay is the place where dogsled races, motorcycles on ice, snowshoers, and snowmobiles can be found. Other features include pancake breakfasts, arts and crafts, and a midway.

usually held the third weekend in February

Muskoka Winter Carnival

Bracebridge, Gravenhurst, and Huntsville

These towns combine their efforts to produce a super winter party. A variety of events fill four days — a spaghetti eating contest, a pie eating contest, log sawing and nail driving competitions, dogsled races, snowshoe races, a tug-of-war, a torchlight parade, a fiddle contest, and square dancing.

usually held from Thursday to Sunday, the third weekend in February

Snow White Winter Carnival

Durham

No wicked witches here, just good food, entertainment, snowmobile races, and a beauty pageant.

usually held the third weekend in February

Winter Carnival

Haliburton

Three fun filled days of winter celebration are found at the Haliburton Winter Carnival. Activities include a parade, bed races, a carnival queen contest, and snowmobile races.

usually held the third weekend in February

Winter Festival

Midland

There are many activities for children and adults at this festival. Tobaggan rides are one of the favourite events.

usually held the third weekend in February

Winterfest

North Bay

Celebrate winter while watching figure skating, cross-country skiing, and free style skiing competitions. This festival also features a mini-carnival and a gymnastics display.

usually held the third weekend in February

Winter Carnival

Burlington — (416) 639-1873

Winter games and a Snow Queen Contest highlight this four day event.

usually held in mid-February

Winter Carnival

Welland — (416) 732-5331

This carnival features snow sculpturing, skating races, hay rides, log sawing, broomball games and a country jamboree.

usually held the last week in January

Winter Carnival

Arthur — (519) 848-2311

This carnival is sponsored by the Lion's Club and features various winter activities.

usually held towards the end of February

Winter Carnival

Kirkland Lake

This festival features all the winter sports plus a torchlight parade, log sawing, donut eating contests, and a Carnival Queen contest.

usually held the last week in February through the first week in March.

Other communities holding **Winter Carnivals** in February include: Bobcaygeon, Brantford, Cloyne, Eganville, Napanee, and Orillia — *usually held the first weekend in February;* Bewdley, Bluevale, Brockville, Cobden, Cochrane, Point Alexander, and Tweed — *usually held the second weekend in February;* Clarence Creek — *usually held the third week in February;* Chapleau, Milton, Parry Sound, Vermilion Bay, and Wawa — *usually held the third weekend in February;* Hearst, Penetanguishene, Port Sydney, Westmeath, and Whitby — *usually held the last weekend in February.*

Blue Mountain Winter Carnival

Collingwood

This winter carnival features games, entertainment, costumes, parades, races, food, and lots of fun.

usually held in mid-March

As the lamb and the lion fight it out, some communities hold their **Winter Carnivals: Iroquois Falls** and **Kapuskasing** — *usually held the first weekend in March;* and **Elk Lake** and **Porquis Junction** — *usually held the second weekend in March.*

Travel notes

Spring

Spring is welcomed in Ontario with sighs of relief. The sun warms the earth, the colours change from grey to green, and a variety of fairs and festivals "spring" up.

Spring is the time for one of Ontario's most popular agricultural events, the maple syrup festival. These festivals are gastronomical extravaganzas of pancakes and syrup, maple sugar candy, and apple fritters. And you can practically let your nose guide you to them with that sweet maple aroma in the fresh, spring air. You can work up an appetite with a tour of the sugarbush, where you'll see how maple products are made.

As well as the spring sap run-off, there's a run-off of the ice and snow that built up all winter. That creates fast flowing rivers, and that means canoe, kayak, and homemade boat races. These races provide breathtaking excitement, excellent picture-taking possibilities, and lots of laughs.

Spring is always a busy time for farm people. There are fields to be ploughed, planting to be done, sheep to be sheared, and young animals to be cared for. But farmers somehow find the time to take part in agricultural fairs. Take one in and maybe you'll be inspired to try out your own green thumb.

Paddyfest

Listowel — (519) 291-2950

Don some green and join the fun at the St. Patrick's Day weekend celebration. Lots of events and green beer, too.

usually held the Thursday, Friday, and Saturday closest to March 17 (St. Patty's Day)

Maple Syrup Festival

Sweabury — (519) 485-2267

Located at the George Jakeman Sugar Shanty and Historic Building, this festival offers pancakes and maple syrup, a craft show and sale, and antique exhibits.

usually held the last weekend in March

Maple Syrup Time

Milton — (416) 878-4131

It's Maple Syrup Time at the Mountsberg Wildlife Centre. There are horse-drawn sleigh and wagon rides, exhibits, and a pancake house.

held during March and April on Saturdays, Sundays and holidays

Maple Syrup Festival

Vineland — (416) 892-2609

Welcome spring with a visit to a Maple Syrup Festival. Vineland's features static and working displays of historic and modern syrup making methods, plus maple syrup products for sale.

held during the entire month of March

Other communities holding sugaring-off celebrations in March include: **Alvinston** ((519) 245-3710); **Aurora** ((416) 895-1281); **Avon** ((519) 631-1270); **Dorset** ((705) 766-2451); **Kleinburg; Maple; Orangeville** ((519) 951-1520); **Orillia; Smiths Falls** ((613) 692-3571); **Stouffville** ((416) 887-5979); **Warsaw** ((705) 745-5791); **Wiarton; and Wingham.**

From tree to table

It takes between thirty and forty gallons of maple tree sap to produce one gallon of maple syrup. So what makes it to your breakfast table is literally the cream of the crop.

Maple sap is the nutrient liquid that stimulates growth in maple trees each spring. It contains only about one to four percent sugar. The syrup that makes it to the table however, contains at least 66 percent sugar and that's what captures the sweet-tooth market. This magical transformation occurs through boiling the sap, filtering it, and collecting the concentrate.

Exactly when the sap starts to flow depends on the weather. Usually, when the cold winter weather breaks, giving us warm, sunny spring days and cool nights, the maple sap begins to flow. In Ontario, this usually occurs over a three to six week period between early March and mid-April.

Anyone who has ever tasted the real thing will assure you that maple syrup bears little resemblance to what is labelled "pancake syrup" or "table syrup" in the supermarkets. Don't be fooled by imitations. In Ontario, the real stuff must be labelled simply "Maple Syrup" or "Pure Maple Syrup."

Syrup in Ontario is graded according to colour and flavour. Number one syrup is a light or medium brown colour and is delicately flavoured. It is primarily for table use. Number two syrup is darker and stronger flavoured, lending itself to use in cooking. Number three syrup is usually used in food processing industries and is not as suitable for the consumer.

It is always a good idea to store containers of maple syrup in the refrigerator or freezer once they have been opened. If containers are sealed, they can be kept for several months in a cool, dry place or for one year in a freezer.

If you purchase syrup in large containers, such as gallon cans, and plan to use it over a long period of time, it is advisable to re-pack it. The syrup should be heated to 85°C (180°F) and then poured into smaller sterilized jars. Seal the jars tightly and let them stand upside down for ten to 15 minutes. Then turn them upright and let them cool. Once cooled, store them in a cool, dry place or a freezer. If you do freeze syrup, it is important to leave an inch or two of space in the jars to allow for expansion.

Many of the maple syrup festivals in Ontario offer tours of the sugarbush and demonstrations of the syrup-making process. Syrup is also available for sale at most of them. Canada is famous for its maple syrup and a trip to a festival will surely show you why.

Maple Syrup Pie

1 unbaked, unpricked 10″ pie shell
2 tbsp. butter
1 cup firmly packed brown sugar
3 egg yolks
1/2 cup milk
1 cup pure maple syrup
freshly grated nutmeg
3 egg whites

Cream together butter and sugar; add the egg yolks and beat well. Stir in the milk, maple syrup, and nutmeg.

Beat the egg whites until they are stiff but not dry, and fold them into the maple syrup mixture. Pour the mixture into the pie shell and bake at 200°C (450°F) for 10 minutes; reduce heat to 195°C (350°F) for 30-35 minutes more or until the filling is set and the crust is golden brown.

Serve this sweet-tooth pleasing pie with whipped cream.

Maple Nut Muffins

one half cup maple syrup
2 tbsp. melted butter
one quarter cup chopped walnuts
2 cups all-purpose flour
3 tbsp. baking powder
1 tsp. salt
1 cup milk
3 tbsp. maple syrup
one quarter cup of salad oil
1 egg

Grease 12 large muffin cups. Put 2 tsp. maple syrup, one half tsp. melted butter and 1 tsp. chopped nuts into each cup. Sift flour, baking powder and salt into a mixing bowl. Mix the remaining ingredients together. Blend this mixture in with the flour mixture, stirring with a fork. Spoon into muffin cups, filling two thirds full. Bake at 220°C (425°F) for 20 minutes. Remove from cups immediately and enjoy.

Maple Syrup Festival

Delta

This spring celebration features tours of sugarbushes, tours of the United Maple Products Packing Plant, and pancakes and syrup.
usually held the first weekend in April

Algoma Maple Syrup Festival

Richard's Landing

This spring festival is dedicated to "sugaring-off". Free tours of sugarbushes are available.
usually held the first weekend in April

Maple Syrup Festival

Wilberforce

Sugaring-off demonstrations, a pancake lunch, a flea market, craft displays, and a dance are the features of this Maple Syrup Festival.
usually held the first weekend in April

Maple Syrup Festival

Woodstock

Woodstock hosts the Annual West Oxford Women's Institute Maple Syrup Festival, featuring modern syrup production, antique and craft displays, craft sales, pancakes and good home baking. Located on George Jackman's Farm, just outside Woodstock.
usually held the first weekend in April

Maple Syrup Festival

Elmira — (519) 669-2605

One of the most popular Maple Syrup Festivals, Elmira's features sugarbush tours, maple syrup making in the pioneer way, a sidewalk mall with over 100 vendors selling crafts, preserves, Mennonite quilts, and of course, maple syrup and maple sugar candy. There's lots of food too — pancakes, apple fritters, and other Pennslyvania-Dutch cuisine. Be sure to arrive early!
held the first Saturday in April (unless that falls during Easter Weekend, as it does in 1980, in which case the festival is held on the last Saturday in March.)

Crazy Boat Race

Milton — (416) 877-3855

Imagine the fun of this race when the only entry requirement is that the boat floats! The course follows the Credit River from Cheltenham to Glen Williams.
usually held the Saturday closest to April Fools Day

Canoe Marathon Race

Seaforth

This spring marathon canoe race, 23 km long, is sponsored by the Optimist Club of Seaforth.
usually held the first Sunday in April

Waterfowl Appreciation Day

Strathroy — (519) 245-3944

Try your skill or have one of the naturalists assist you in identifying waterfowl and shorebirds.
usually held the first Sunday in April.

Annual Antique Show

Guelph — (519) 821-3611

Housed in the Centennial Arena, this two-day show of antiques reflects this town's past.
usually held the second weekend in April

Maple Syrup Festival

Belmore — (519) 335-3604

Belmore's festival features maple syrup-making demonstrations, tours of the sugarbushes, and home baking including pancakes and sausages, and of course, maple syrup.
usually held the second Saturday in April

Maple Syrup Festival

Watford — (519) 876-3636

Take a bus from town out to the sugarbush at Campbell Conservation Area and watch the syrup-making process. Attractions in town include pancakes and sausages, home baking, crafts, and maple syrup sales.
usually held the second Saturday in April

Spring Surprise Cycling Rally

Burlington — (416) 689-6126

Bicycles are a sure sign of spring! And here's a chance to combine exercise and family fun. This family rally and picnic begins at Hidden Valley Park at 9:30 a.m. There is a registration fee.
usually held the second Sunday in April

Algonquin Maple Syrup Festival

Sundridge — (705) 384-5567

Everything you always wanted to know about maple syrup can be discovered at the Maple Syrup Museum in a log cabin atmosphere. There are demonstrations and maple products are for sale.
held daily, late March through early April with a special festival day on the second Sunday in April

Dance of the Woodcock

Windsor

Have you ever been unable to sleep at night for pondering the courting habits of birds? End those sleepless nights with a visit to Ojibway Park. This spring hike will uncover the mysteries of the courtship flights of woodcocks, owls and other birds.

usually held the second week in April, depending, of course, on the amorous mood of the birds

Maple Syrup Festival

Elmvale

One of your last chances to attend a Maple Syrup Festival this year! The Elmvale celebration has sugarbush tours, entertainment, a midway, street booths, and all the pancakes and maple syrup you can eat!

usually held on the third Saturday in April

Maple Fest

Parry Sound

This Maple Syrup Festival has a native people's slant: there are trapping and pelt displays; snowshoe making demonstrations; native crafts and foods, music and dancing. Maple syrup related activities include trips to the sugarbush, old fashioned and modern syrup making displays, and maple syrup sales.

usually held the first Friday and Saturday in April

Festival of the Maples

Perth

An entire day of Maple Syrup activities! Start the day with a hearty breakfast of sausages and pancakes with maple syrup. Then visit a sugarbush and watch maple syrup being made. Return to town and stroll through 60 arts and crafts booths, an antique car display, all while listening to live country music. Enjoy a buffalo BBQ and in the evening dance to country music at the community hall.

usually held the third Saturday in April

Sydenham Canoe Race

Strathroy — (519) 245-3710

This canoe race is 24 km long and goes from the Melwood Conservation Area to Alvinston. It features both kayaks and canoes.

usually held on the third Sunday in April

Fiddleheads

Picture the end of a violin, the part where the pegs are, and you'll have a pretty good idea of what fiddleheads look like.

Fiddleheads are a spring delicacy found in damp forests, usually amidst cedars, or near river banks. They are unopened ferns; it's hard to believe that they become lush, plume-like leaves that blanket many Ontario forests throughout the summer.

Fiddleheads can be collected only for a few weeks in May. Pinch off the tight, green coils, leaving no more than an inch or so of stem. Rinse them well in several changes of cold water to remove all traces of their brown papery covering.

Fiddleheads make a unique and tasty addition to any spring meal. They can be prepared in a variety of ways: steamed and served as a vegetable with lemon and butter; marinated and tossed in a green salad; baked in the oven with mild cheese; and even pickled.

Try this recipe should you acquire an abundance of fiddleheads:

Fiddlehead Pickles

Rinse fiddleheads well, making sure to remove all traces of grit and that brown papery covering. Boil for 10 minutes in 2 changes of slightly salted water. Drain well and pack into sterilized jars. To each jar add this mixture, which has boiled 5 minutes: 1 tbsp. sugar, 1/2 tsp. each of salt, dry tarragon, and celery seed, 1/4 cup water and 3/4 cup white vinegar. Seal the jars and store for at least one month. This recipe makes 2, 16 oz. jars of pickles.

A jar of these homemade Fiddlehead Pickles makes a terrific Christmas present.

Mennonite Festival of the Arts

Waterloo

Held at the Conestoga Mall, this art festival exhibits work by both professional and amateur craftsmen. There's a large display of quilts, demonstrations of weaving and silkscreening, Mennonite choirs, and traditional Mennonite refreshments. There are no sales at this show.

usually held the last Sunday in April, 1 p.m. to 6 p.m.

Elora Gorge Whitewater Race

Elora

Spend the whole weekend enjoying canoe fun! Saturday, take in the West Montrose Canoe Race; Sunday watch the experts (and almost experts) battle the foaming whitewater course through Elora's scenic gorge. Lots of opportunities for breath-taking pictures, so bring your camera.

usually held the fourth Sunday in April

Waterloo County Cycling Tour

Kitchener — (519) 689-6126

Starting from Wilson Park at 9 a.m., this cycling tour takes you through a historic, picturesque region. There is a registration fee.
usually held the last Sunday in April.

Beaver Valley River Rat Races

Thornbury

Leave the rat-race of the city and head for a River-Rat-Race! Watch the hilarious antics of men and women in their bathtubs and homemade boats.

Remember your camera to capture all the wild costumes and unique floating vehicles.

There's a craft show in town, too.

The race starts just south of Thornbury, in Heathcote.
usually held the fourth Sunday in April

Antique Show and Sale

Fort Erie — (416) 871-3167

This show and sale features antique furniture, glass, and china.
usually held the end of April

River-rats

If Huck Finn were alive today, he'd probably paddle his raft north to Ontario each spring to enter it in the Beaver River-Rat Boat Race. It's that spirit of adventure and fun that dominates this annual event.

The race is held in April, when many people have to face similar fast rushing waters with sandbags and determination. It begins on the Beaver River at Heathcote and ends at Clarksburg. It attracts several hundred competitors each year, including some from the United States.

There are few rules in the race and even those that do exist are sometimes stretched. Boats must be homemade, have one flat end less than 2 feet square in area, and have at least 2 crew members. The most important rule in the race cannot be stretched; all contestants must wear life jackets.

Speed is not the only consideration in the River-Rat Boat Race. Competitors take special pride in their boats, and their inventiveness is limited only by their imaginations. Almost anything will float if you strap something buoyant to it. Inner tubes, oil drums, plastic bottles, and pieces of styrofoam are among the most common flotation devices.

Portability is one of the primary considerations when building a boat for this event. Competitors must portage over the Clendenon Dam along the route. They must also contend with initially launching the boat, and seasoned observers say that this is one of the most entertaining parts of the race to watch. A bonus for spectators in the past has been that some competitors have donned outfits to match crafts such as pirate and viking ships. Fortunately, there are many good vantage points along the Beaver Valley Road.

The combination of fast rushing, cold water and some less than seaworthy crafts makes safety an important factor. Scuba divers are positioned at regular intervals along the route to aid those who capsize and help recover their boats. There are also officials equipped with ropes and other life saving equipment on hand. In the event of injuries, there is an ambulance standing by.

You could read Mark Twain's Huckleberry Finn each year, to try and get into the spirit of summer. But if you don't have the inclination to read and want to achieve the same feeling, why not head for Heathcote and get your feet wet? Huck would approve.

Blossom Festival

Niagara Falls — (416) 356-2521

Be sure to find the time to take in the beauty of the colours, and the delicate fragrance of the spring blossoms of the Niagara region. Events during this four-week festival include a parade, flower show and competition, international police tug-of-war, and arts and crafts shows.

usually held the last week of April through the third week of May, as the trees bloom

Spring Planting

Oakville — (416) 827-6911

Watch spring planting, done with the aid of horse-drawn equipment, at the Bronte Creek Provincial Park.

daily, late April until mid-May

Glenhyrst Gardens Antique Show and Sale

Brantford — (519) 756-5932

Collectors from all over Ontario consider this show and sale to be one of the best and most interesting shows; see if they're right. A gourmet buffet lunch is available.

usually held Wednesday to Friday, during the first week of May

Prima Festa

Guelph — (519) 822-8630

This Italian Festival features a bocci tournament, a bicycle race, Italian food, dancing, and music.

usually held the first week of May

Festival of the Arts

Ingersoll — (519) 485-4930

In the land of cheddar cheese, this festival brings craftsmen and musicians together.

usually held the first weekend in May

Dundas Valley Bicycle Tour

Dundas — (416) 335-3426

Cycle your troubles away in the pretty Dundas Valley. The tour leaves from the Dundas Centre in the morning; there is a registration fee.

usually held the first Sunday in May

Spring Hike

Exeter — (519) 235-2610

Put on your hiking boots and head out to the Morrison Dam Conservation Area for this guided Spring Hike.

usually held the first Sunday in May

Spring Wild Flowers

Poplar Hill — (519) 245-3710

Learn how to identify wild flowers at the Coldstream Conservation Area. Guides are available to assist budding naturalists.

usually held the first Sunday in May

Stanhope Fly-in and Air Show

Stanhope (Twp. in Haliburton County)

Land vehicles are welcome too at this huge display of new and vintage aircraft, model airplanes, and antique cars. A beef barbecue lunch is available.

usually held the second Sunday in May

Spring wild flowers

There are a few different approaches and aids available to you for discovering this season's wild flowers: most Ontario Provincial and National parks have lists of the wild flowers found there; many naturalist clubs have guided hikes and tours; or get yourself a good book, such as *Peterson's Guide to Wild Flowers of North America*, or *Katherine Mackenzie's Wild Flowers of Eastern Canada*, and see what you can uncover on your own.

Keep in mind these friendly words of advice: some wild flowers, or parts of them, are poisonous — if you're not sure, don't eat it!; paint, photograph or just gaze at, instead of picking, the flowers — but if you must pick, do not over-pick and take the last flower of an area.

Here are a few species to get you started:

Marsh Marigold

Watch the ditches and roadside marshes while driving in the country — you're bound to spot a mass of these large, golden yellow flowers. The leaves can be cooked and eaten, and its roots were sometimes used medicinally.

Trillium

The trillium, Ontario's official floral emblem, blooms in the late spring and early summer. The plant is usually a foot tall with three large petals that are either white, red, or white and red. You should never pick trilliums. Trilliums have been used for folk medicines. The roots can be used to treat stomach disorders, rheumatism, and earaches.

The Common Blue Violet

There's nothing common about this wild flower other than its abundance. It has many uses, as well as being delightful to look at. The leaves can be used raw in salads, or sautéed and folded into an omlette. The flowers can be made into delicate candies, floated in cocktails, or tossed in a salad. The Common Blue Violet has a five petal blue flower, and heart shaped leaves; it blooms in late spring and early summer.

Hepatica

Watch for white, pink, lavender, or blue hepatica flowers. You'll find them in early spring in heavily wooded areas. Some of them have a sweet smell, and you'll be delighted when you find one that does!

Skunk Cabbage

Avoid the leaves of Skunk Cabbage — if they're crushed you'll quickly learn how this wild flower got its name! It is one of the first plants to appear in the spring, blooming even while the snow is still on the ground. The leaves are large and the flower is a deep purple colour, with yellow streaks.

Trout Lily

You're sure to spot the trout lily during spring hikes through the woods. This short plant has a lovely yellow flower between two long, spotted leaves. Cows like to eat the leaves, and they were used by the Indians, brewed as a tea, to help relieve stomach pains.

Anniversary of the Burning of Dover Mills

Port Dover

This festival celebrates (?) the fire of May 18, 1814. An old time military parade (no motors) is a main attraction.

usually held the Sunday closest to May 18

Festival of Spring

Ottawa

This festival originated when Queen Juliana of the Netherlands donated thousands of tulip bulbs to the city. Although it is no longer called the Tulip Festival, thousands of these bright, multi-coloured flowers adorn The Driveway and The Central Experimental Farm. The festival itself is held in Major's Hill Park and features a huge craft market, a beer garden, and daily entertainment.

usually held for two weeks in mid-May

Kintoria Day

Wilberforce

This one day festival features a giant auction, beer garden, and the Kintoria Ball.

usually held the third Saturday in May

Spring Festival of Antiques & and Crafts

Seaforth

The Blythe Community Centre is the scene of this annual event.

usually held the third Saturday in May

Annual Antique and Craft Show

Markdale

Be sure to take in this show and sale, held annually at the Centre Grey Recreation Complex.

usually held the third weekend in May

Voyageur Days

Port Elgin

Step back in time to the days of coonskin caps and exploration. Voyageur Days feature canoe races, barbecues, a street dance and carnival.
usually held the third weekend in May

Spring Fair

Richmond Hill

You'll hardly believe such a country atmosphere could exist so close to Toronto. Spring is declared here with horse, cattle, sheep, poultry, and rabbit shows, crafts, and a Fair Queen Contest.
usually held the third weekend in May

Portugese Fest

West Lorne

Join in this ethnic celebration which featues a colourful parade and dancing.
usually held the third weekend in May

Victoria Day Festival

Fort Erie — (416) 871-0830

Fort Erie celebrates this occasion with rides, games, and fireworks, all sponsored by the local Jaycees.
usually held Victoria Day weekend

Victoria Day Celebration

Jarvis

The Jarvis festivities include a parade, a horse show, rides, games, an amateur show, barbecues, a skydiving display, and of course, Victoria Day fireworks.
held Victoria Day weekend

Victoria Day Celebration

Stoney Creek — (416) 689-6126

Celebrate summer's arrival. This festival features a soap box derby, a stage show, and a huge fireworks display.
held on Victoria Day

Victoria Day Celebration

Woodstock — (519) 539-1291

Southside park is the site for displays, fireworks and family fun.
held Victoria Day

Tulip Festival

Drayton — (519) 669-2605

Celebrate the floral splendour at Drayton's Tulip Festival. Featured are tulip displays, tulip quilts, a Tulip Queen Contest, ethnic dancers, step dancers, and Dutch cuisine and music.
usually held the last Saturday in May

Ontario Mennonite Relief Sale

New Hamburg — (519) 745-4417

Over 300 hand-sewn quilts are auctioned off at this sale. Other traditional Mennonite items which are available include pies, pastries, jams, jellies, pickles and relishes, hooked and braided rugs, stuffed dolls, and afghans. There is also an auction of antiques and household items.

All proceeds from the sale go towards international relief and agricultural development in over 40 countries.
usually held the last Saturday in May

Optimfest

Seaforth

A fun-filled day of dancing, games, and a beef and pork barbecue.
usually held the last Saturday in May

Spring Fair

Schomberg

This agricultural fair features a horse pull, a tractor pull and crafts.
usually held the fourth weekend in May

Festival City Days

Stratford — (519) 271-5140

The whole town joins in the festivities; there's a parade, dance, sidewalk sales, and entertainment for all ages.
usually held the fourth weekend in May

Family Carnival Days

Brussels

Attractions at this carnival include a midway, a trash-to-treasure sale, country and bluegrass music, and a street dance.
usually held the last weekend in May

Kinsmen Carnival

Cambridge

Rides, candy floss, and games of chance mean fun for everyone.
usually held the last weekend in May

Spring Festival

Harrow — (519) 738-2029

Help celebrate the planting of the crops at the John Richardson Park Homestead, County Road 50 and Iler Road.
usually held the last weekend in May

Fish Derby

Kagawong, Manitoulin Island

Prizes are given for the largest perch caught, but a fish fry supper makes everybody a winner.
usually held the last weekend in May

Kent County Exhibition

Chatham — (519) 352-5820

This agricultural fair features a wide variety of displays.
usually held the last week in May

Folk Arts Festival

St. Catharines — (416) 685-6589

Twenty-nine area ethnic clubs produce this festival of arts and crafts, concerts, singing and dancing, and old world folk music.
this festival lasts two weeks, usually from late May to early June

Kawartha Lakes Arts Festival

Lindsay

Ten communities from Victoria County get together to bring you this exciting arts festival, which spans three weeks.
usually held from late May through early June

Sheep to Shawl Festival

Oakville — (416) 827-6911

Find out how your favourite wooly sweater came to be. Sheep Shearing and wool making demonstrations take place at the Spruce Lane Farm, Bronte Creek Provincial Park.
usually held in late May

Spring Fair

Brooklin

Features at this spring agricultural fair include an old time fiddling contest, horse, cattle and sheep shows, a beauty contest and a tug-of-war. Delicious homemade burgers and fries are available.
usually held the first weekend in June

A stitch in time

Quilts are proof that necessity is the mother of invention. For economic and geographic reasons, nothing was wasted on the pioneer homestead. Most clothing was sewn at home, and any leftover material saved, to be one day pieced into a warm and lovely quilt.

Quilts can be a form of family history-keeping. Many of the pieces of fabric kindle a memory for some family member: "This is from that dress I wore to Irene's wedding." Family stories, quilts, and scrap bags are often passed down through generations.

While quilts themselves had much to do with families, the act of quilting was a community event. Quilting bees were a country tradition that gave people a break from everyday chores and a chance to catch up on local news, otherwise known as gossip. Quilting bees were usually held in summer, between the planting and harvest seasons. A quilting frame was usually set up on a verandah, or under the shade of a large tree. Quilts were usually started and finished on the same day. In the evening, the men would arrive, and eating, singing, and dancing would begin to celebrate the productive day.

Names for quilt designs came from everyday rural sights — Log Cabin, Straight Furrow, Barn Raising, Path Through the Woods, Butterfly, and Red Peony for example. Pattern designs were exchanged and copied and many new designs emerged from the materials in the scrap bag.

Today, quilting is still practiced, and quilting bees are still held, though less frequently. In Ontario, Mennonite country is the best place to find old and new quilts. The largest quilting event is the Mennonite Relief Sale, held in late May in New Hamburg.

Should you decide to buy a quilt, here are some tips to keep in mind. Flea markets, auctions, country stores, garage sales, and even attics and storage areas in homes of friends and relatives are good places to look. And remember, it's not really worth buying if you don't like the pattern and colours. With old quilts, check for damage and decide whether you can repair it yourself. Don't let dirt or stains put you off — you can wash old quilts if you're careful. Wash them in the bathtub with warm water and mild suds. Do not wring the quilt — hang it to dry with supports. A sturdy tree branch, out of strong sunlight, might be a good drying place.

If you'd like to try making your own quilt, there are many pattern books available in both traditional and modern designs. Maybe you'll be inspired to try this relaxing, therapeutic craft.

Travel notes

Summer

The lazy, hazy, crazy days of summer have a fair or festival for everyone. There are food fairs and fun fairs, gemborees and jamborees, fiddlers and dancers, buyers and sellers, ethnics and natives, and watchers and doers. Candy floss, foot-longs, and ferris wheels are the order of the day in small towns across Ontario.

Most of the events are held on weekends and many are only a short drive away from Ontario's major cities. If you're stuck in the city during the week, a weekend trip to a fair is a great way to get away from it all.

Lying in the sun can be nice, but there's so much more to do when you are at the cottage. So if you're getting a little bored, change the pace with a visit to a fair. It's a great way to meet your neighbours, and a sure-fire cure for an overdose of peace and quiet.

Bluegrass Canada

Carlisle — (416) 689-5708

Grab a cowboy hat and head out to Courtcliffe Park for a weekend of country and bluegrass music. Top names from Canada and the U.S. perform in concert and workshop settings. This festival also features square dancing and craft displays. Camping facilities are available. Tickets for this weekend of fun are available in advance or at the site.
usually held the first weekend in June

Spring Fair

Clinton — (519) 482-7502

Good country feelings are all around at this agricultural fair. Events include livestock judging, horse, cattle, and sheep shows, crafts, home baking, and a midway.
usually held the first weekend in June

Kinsmen Mudcat Festival

Dunnville — (416) 774-7380

Mudcats (a.k.a. catfish) are the *raison d'etre* for this festival which features a canoe fishing contest, greasy pole climbing contest, bed races, canoe races, a mammoth fish fry, and a dance.
usually held the first weekend in June

Antique Car Days

Kitchener — (519) 744-5382

Two days of antique cars at Doon Pioneer Village — Saturday there's a flea market of used car parts; Sunday there's a display of antique cars.
usually held the first weekend in June

Bluegrass

It's a long way from the blue grass area of Kentucky to Ontario. Yet the music that takes its name from that region is still thriving at Ontario bluegrass festivals in towns like Hillsburgh and Carlisle.

Live performances and festivals have long been the mainstay of bluegrass music, much to the chagrin of record companies struggling to boost sagging sales. This phenomenon probably has much to do with the nature of the music. It has evolved to be an energetic, cheerful, and humourous brand of music that lends itself to foot stompin' and dancin'. And who wants to do that sitting at home alone in front of a stereo system? Bluegrass is music that must be shared to be enjoyed to the fullest — and that's why it's so popular when it's live.

Bluegrass did not always have such an up-tempo sound. The first bluegrass band ever didn't even have a banjo player until Earl Scruggs joined them in 1945. The band was called Bill Monroe and his Blue Grass Boys, and since their inception, music like theirs has become known as bluegrass. Monroe's band featured songs with mournful harmonies and emotional stories about love and death.

Bluegrass music has undergone many changes since the early days of Bill Monroe. Along with a more light-hearted lyrical approach, it now shows influences of folk, jazz, and blues. Some bluegrass purists are disappointed with the changes that have taken place and suggest that the heartfelt, emotional approach to singing has been replaced by slick instrumental prowess. But as long as searing fiddle and banjo solos get the crowds on their feet, the trend will likely continue.

If you think there's nothing more to bluegrass than the theme to the Beverley Hillbillies television show and Dueling Banjos, a festival should change your mind.

Historical Show and Steam Festival

Norwich — (519) 863-2213

Come and see machinery from a bygone era. There are working displays of restored steam engines and tractors, antique cars, plus crafts and a midway.

usually held the first weekend in June

Sail Past and Fish Fry

Port Colborne

First a sail past of Colborne's fishing fleet in full regalia, then a fish fry along the canal banks.

usually held the first weekend in June

Bread and Honey Festival

Streetsville

Arts and crafts, parades, music, and dancing are all part of this festival, held at the Streetsville Memorial Park.

usually held the first weekend in June

Annual Uxbridge Stampede

Uxbridge

Enjoy all the excitement of a rodeo, without going to Calgary.

usually held the first weekend in June

Art in the Park

Windsor

Willistead Park is the site of this arts and crafts show.

usually held the first weekend in June

Summerfest

Acton

This town celebrates the arrival of summer with crafts, singing, bands, and live theatre at the Acton High School.

usually held the first Saturday in June

Summer Arts Festival

Georgetown — (416) 877-4078

Arts and crafts, folk singing, bands, and choral groups make this a sight and sound festival.

usually held the first Saturday in June

Arts and Crafts Show

Orangeville — (519) 941-0822

There are over 45 craftsmen and artists displaying and selling their work at this show, which is sponsored by the Women's Division of the Orangeville Agricultural Society.

usually held the first Saturday in June

Mayfest

Prescott — (613) 925-2343

This festival, sponsored by the Kinsmen, features concerts and beer gardens.

usually held the first Saturday in June

Pedal to the Pines

Sarnia

Join in this cycling tour from Centennial Park to the Pinery Provincial Park.

usually held the first Saturday in June

Canada Flag Day

Stoney Creek — (416) 561-4534

This celebration features a pancake breakfast, art in the park, beer gardens, a cake decorating contest, a street dance and a parade.

usually held the first Saturday in June

Family Day at Glenhyrst

Brantford — (519) 756-5932

Marching bands and craft displays make this a fun family outing.

usually held the first Sunday in June

Blessing of the Boats

Port Perry

Plan to be part of this unique waterfront service at the Port Perry Yacht Club.

usually held on the first Sunday in June

Antique Show and Sale

Wallaceburg — (519) 627-5720

This annual event draws both dealers and collectors.

usually held weekdays, during the latter half of the second week in June

Agricultural Festival

Aurora

This fair has competitions for heavy horses, ponies, hunters and jumpers. And a midway, too!

usually held the second weekend in June

Annual Flea Market

Brussels — (519) 887-9216

You're sure to find "just what you've always been looking for" at this flea market. There's also an antique car show and a vintage aircraft show.

usually held the second weekend in June

Textile Festival

Cambridge (Hespeler) — (519) 658-9311

Discover the hows and whys of the wool world — take a tour through a wool weaving factory. Other features of this festival include a textile and craft exhibition, quilting competitions, and weaving, sewing, and quilting demonstrations. There is a festival parade, food booths, and a midway.

usually held the second weekend in June

Folklore Festival

Kingston

This three day multi-cultural festival features ethnic pavilions with food, music and dancing.

usually held the second weekend in June

Scottish Weekend

Kitchener — (519) 744-5382

Celebrate Scottish traditions at the Doon Pioneer Village with highland dancing, music, crafts and Scottish food.

usually held the second weekend in June

Summer Fair

Millbrook

This agricultural fair is bound to be a winner. Cattle, horse, poultry and rabbit shows, a horse pull, and tractor pulls are just some of the events.

usually held the second weekend in June

St. Anne's Festival

St. Thomas

St. Anne's Parish hosts this festival which features a celebrated bake sale.

usually held the second weekend in June

Beef Barbecue and Dance

Clinton — (519) 482-7502

Good country food and fun!

usually held the second Saturday in June

Speyside Highland Games

Georgetown — (416) 877-4431

Kilts, bagpipes, dancing, caber tossing — that's what highland games are made of.

usually held the second Saturday in June

Lobsterfest

Sarnia

Grab your bib and claw-crackers — it's time for the Annual Rotary Lobsterfest!

usually held the second Sunday in June

Arts and Crafts Show

Seaforth — (519) 527-0108

Over 50 exhibitors, displaying a wide variety of arts and crafts, participate in this annual event.

usually held the second Saturday in June

Waterloo Days

Waterloo — (519) 886-1550

Enjoy the wide variety of events — sporting, cultural and musical activities for all ages.
usually held the second and third weekends in June

Carrousel of the Nations

Windsor — (519) 255-1127

Over 30 ethnic groups produce this festival of cooking, entertainment, dancing and sports events.
usually held the second and third weekends in June

Town and Country Fair

Burlington — (416) 634-7731

As the name implies, this festival combines the best of both worlds. There's an ethnic village, horse shows, entertainment and amusement rides.
usually held in mid-June

Welland Rose Festival

Welland

This annual horticultural event celebrates the prize-winning roses of the Welland area. Events include rose shows and competitions, a Rose Queen Contest, parades, boat races, an aquatic show and a Coronation Ball. A rose is a rose is a rose.
usually held in mid-June

Annual Flower Festival

Brampton

This week-long festival includes a huge variety of activities, including flower shows, arts and crafts, pet show, beauty pageant, sporting events, dances, and barbecues.
usually held the third week in June

Udder nonsense

With the rising cost of dairy products, you may be considering buying a cow. And just so you'll know what you're getting, a good cow, well fed and cared for, should produce about 3600 litres of milk a year. That should be enough to keep you chugging with some left over to make butter and cheese. However, before going into the dairy business, you should also consider that cows eat between 19 and 24 pounds of hay per day.

If a cow doesn't suit you, how about a goat? A good goat can produce 2 or 3 litres of milk a day for 8 to 10 months and can be fed for less than 20% of what it costs to feed a cow. And furthermore, a good milk-giving goat usually costs less than $100 to begin with.

Spring Fair

Hensall

This agricultural fair features horse and calf shows, and craft and cooking displays.
usually held on Tuesday during the third week in June

Summer Fair

Maxville

This major agricultural fair features the Eastern Ontario Regional Holstein Show, plus horse shows and hitches.
usually held Thursday, Friday and Saturday, the third week in June

Rotorama

Milton — (416) 878-7184

There's something for everyone at Milton's Rotorama. Choose from events such as fiddle contests, horse shows, model plane competitions, musical rides, and beer gardens.
usually held Wednesday to Saturday, the third week in June

Jug Band Festival

Exeter

Relax to the sounds of real country jug bands at the Recreation Centre.
usually held the third weekend in June

Burgerfest

Grand Bend — (519) 238-2001

Bed races, a foot race, canoe races, sky diving, and a craft show all lead up to a burger feast on the beach.
usually held the third weekend in June

Ontario's Fiddle Contest

Hensall — (519) 262-2812

See and hear fiddlers from across Canada and the U.S. as they compete for cash prizes. There is also a step-dance contest, and a wind-up dance for participants and spectators alike. Camping is available.
usually held the third weekend in June

Sidewalk Art Show

Niagara-On-The-Lake — (416) 468-7177

Why not pick up something for that bare wall? The work of local artists is on display from noon til dusk.

usually held the third weekend in June

Craft Show and Sale

Owen Sound — (519) 376-3226

Georgian Bay artisans display and sell their work at this annual event.

usually held the third weekend in June

Milling Days

Port Rowan — (519) 586-2201

Backus Conservation Area is the site of this display of early flour making methods. Why not take a sack of stone ground flour home? There is also a log-sawing demonstration.

usually held the third weekend in June

Back 40 Bluegrass Festival

Woodstock — (519) 539-5815

Head out to the Pittock Conservation Area for this bluegrass festival and competition.

usually held the third weekend in June

Spring Festival

Kitchener — (519) 745-2531

Bingeman Park is the place to be to see demonstrations of ethnic cooking and arts and crafts. Entertainment is also provided.

usually held the third Saturday in June

Highland Games

Port Elgin — (519) 832-2332

Located in the heart of the only county in Canada with its own registered tartan — Bruce County — these highland games should be high on your list of "must-attend" things this summer. There are pipeband competitions, dancing competitions, a tug-of-war, a heptathon, and a dance in the evening. There's shuttlebus service available between all events and dances, downtown, the beach, and parking lots.

usually held the third Saturday in June

Kids' Day

Sault Ste. Marie

Kids will love the parade and contests at the Memorial Gardens.

usually held the third Saturday in June

Canadian Open Square and Step Dancing Competition

Dundalk

Watch young and old contestants from far and near compete for prizes. Maybe you'll even pick up some pointers to improve your own dancing style!

usually held Friday and Saturday, the fourth weekend in June

Cactus Festival

Dundas — (416) 526-6328

Watch where you sit during the Cactus Festival! Festivities include a carnival, bed races, a parade, and a casino dance in the arena.

usually held the last weekend in June

Antique, Flower and Art Show and Sale

Durham

Find an antique vase and flowers to fill it at this combination show and sale.

usually held Friday and Saturday, the last weekend in June

Annual Stratford Festival Bicycle Tour

Paris — (519) 442-6235

This is a two-day excursion which covers about 224 km (140 miles). There is overnight accommodation provided. It starts Saturday at the Paris post office. There is a registration fee.

usually held the last weekend in June

Frontier Days

Parkhill — (519) 294-6256

Return to the old fashioned days of sheriffs and jails through parades, dances, a giant beef barbecue, and talent shows.

usually held the fourth weekend in June

Old Time Fiddlers' Contest

Petrolia — (519) 882-2350

This age-old art comes alive here.

usually held Friday and Saturday, fourth weekend in June

Art-In-The-Park

Belleville

There's more than just arts and crafts at this fair — square dancing, canoe races and kite flying are also on hand for family enjoyment.

usually held the last Saturday in June

Bugle and Drum Band Parade

Kingsville — (519) 733-2315

Entrants from Canada and the U.S. participate in this parade and competition. Another attraction is the Kinsmen Soap Box Derby.

usually held the last Saturday in June

Artists and Crafts Festival

Komoka — (519) 471-2445

This popular show includes artisans and craftsmen displaying weaving, leather work, woodwork, needlepoint, painting, jewellery, and ceramics.

usually held the last Saturday in June

Heritage Day

Alvinston

Tours of the historic museum house, crafts, and antique car displays celebrate this region's heritage. It's at the A.W. Campbell Conservation Area.

usually held the fourth Sunday in June

Strawberry Social

Burlington

The Joseph Brant Museum is the site for this strawberry day. There's entertainment, special museum displays, and of course, strawberry sundaes.

usually held the last Sunday in June

Friends of the Museum Festival

Milton

Children will love participating in games from the 1800s, one of the attractions of this festival. There are also demonstrations of early crafts and musical entertainment. It all takes place at the Halton Regional Museum, in the Kelso Conservation Area.

usually held the fourth Sunday in June

Multi-Cultural Festival

Guelph

Ethnic foods, dancing and music are featured in this two-week long celebration.

usually held late June through early July

Canadian Lakehead Exhibition

Thunder Bay

This major agricultural fair is known throughout northern Ontario for its horse, dairy and beef cattle shows, craft demonstrations and entertainment.

held for 10 days, usually at the end of June

Many communities across the province celebrate Canada Day with music, dancing, and fireworks. Some of those communities are: **Alexandria (613) 525-2084; Aurora; Barry's Bay; Beamsville (416) 563-8205; Brantford; Cornwall (613) 445-6453; Fort Erie; Goderich (519) 524-6600; Grimsby (416) 945-3519; Harrow (519) 738-2029; Harrowsmith; Kincardine (519) 395-5180; Kingston; Manitouwadge; Milton (416) 878-3179; Niagara Falls; Owen Sound; Port Stanley (519) 782-3264; Renfrew; Sarnia (519) 336-5049; Sioux Narrows (807) 226-3293; and Wallaceburg (519) 627-2640.**

Highland Games

Embro

Spend this holiday surrounded by Scottish heritage. Traditional bagpipe music, dancing, and food create the highland atmosphere.

usually held on Canada Day

Calithumpian Parade

Port Dover

Celebrate the holiday here with antique cars, a tug-of-war, a sailboat race, and a local talent show.

usually held Canada Day

Back to Acton Days

Acton

With Acton's main street converted to a pedestrian mall, it's easy to get involved in the festivities.

usually held on the July 1 holiday weekend

Festival of Flowers

Belleville

It's every flower for himself when the judges cast a critical eye towards the various categories on display at the Festival of Flowers.

usually held the July 1 holiday weekend

Festival of the Woodland Indian

Brantford

Why not spend Canada Day with the country's original inhabitants? Native performers entertain with traditional singing, dancing, and drama. Native foods and crafts are also available.

usually held on the July 1 holiday weekend

Pioneer Days

Brockville — (613) 342-6553

This will take you back to the days of bustles and buggies! Events include square dancing, canoe races, a soapbox derby, a fishing derby, a carnival and a parade.

usually held the July 1 holiday weekend

Summerfest

Chapleau

Lumberjack and railroad competitions highlight this festival which also includes a midway.

usually held the July 1 holiday weekend

Native Indian Pow-Wow

Delaware

Enjoy the colour and pageantry of ancestral dancing and drumming. Native arts and crafts are featured as well.

usually held the July 1 weekend

Uranium Festival

Elliot Lake — (705) 848-2287

This festival features mucking and drilling competitions, a soapbox derby, a midway, a beer garden and a parade.

usually held the July 1 holiday weekend

Fun in the Sun Festival

Fort Frances

There's enough to keep even the smallest attention span occupied — a two-day canoe race, a marathon swim, sky-diving, a bathtub derby, log rolling, and a midway. There is also a Native people's display and pow-wow.

usually held July 1 holiday weekend

Lake of the Woods Folk Festival

Kenora

Head up north for this festival of bluegrass, country and folk music. There's also a **Multi-Cultural Festival,** which features ethnic music and food.

both are usually held the July 1 holiday weekend

The Great Steamboat Race

Kingston

This is an annual gathering of steamships from many North American ports. Events include relays, races, and an obstacle course.

usually held the July 1 holiday weekend

Homecoming Weekend

Mindemoya, Manitoulin Island

Festivities here include a fiddling contest, a horseshoe tournament, a horse show, and a tractor pull. There are pancake breakfasts and fish-fry suppers too.

usually held the July 1 holiday weekend

Old Home Week

Morrisburg — (613) 543-2851

Arts and crafts, a midway, music, sports events, and a parade are some of the features of this festival.

usually held the week of July 1

Niagara Antique Power Show

Port Colborne

Capture the fascinating era of steam and early internal combustion engines. There are tractors, sawmills, antique cars and farm machinery in working displays.

usually held the July 1 holiday weekend

Frontier Days

Port Elgin

This town's Canada Day Celebrations include a rodeo, a beef barbecue and a dance.

usually held the July 1 holiday weekend

Arts and Crafts Show

Ridgetown

This show and sale features demonstrations of wood carving, painting, pottery, and macrame.

usually held the July 1 holiday weekend

Settler's Days

Smiths Falls

Celebrate the 1867 founding of this country in the spirit of that time. Events include pancake breakfasts, historical displays, bed races, horse shows, bluegrass music, children's games, and fireworks.

usually held July 1 holiday weekend

Charcoal Festival

South River

A parade, fireworks, and dancing help to celebrate the days when the wealth of this area was wood.

usually held the July 1 holiday weekend

Holidayfest

West Lorne

There's music for all tastes here — polka, waltz, and rock. Munch on various delights from ethnic food stands as you enjoy the tunes.

usually held on the July 1 holiday weekend

Fiddle Contest and Step-Dance Contest

Wilberforce

The name says it all.

usually held the July 1 holiday weekend

International Freedom Festival

Windsor — (519) 252-7264

Windsor's Canada week celebrations are extended to include the Americans' Independence Day. The combination produces a smashing festival that features a huge fireworks display, sporting events, arts and crafts, and much more.

held from the last week of June through to July 4

Pioneer Festival

Kitchener — (519) 576-5000

Pioneer activities, displays, and crafts are featured at the Doon Pioneer Village.

usually held in early July

Homecoming Weekend

Port Dover

Surf and turf activities — tug boat, trawler and sailboat races, a band tatoo, and one of the oldest parades in Canada make Port Dover home to all.

usually held in early July

Chicken Bar-B-Q

Mitchell — (519) 348-8429

Enjoy savoury chicken at this outdoor dinner.

usually held Wednesday of the first week in July

Annual Antique Show and Sale

Owen Sound

Everyone's bound to find something at this three-day show and sale held at the Owen Sound Arena.

usually held Thursday to Saturday, first week in July

Annual Craft and Hobby Fair

Port Elgin — (519) 934-2925

This fair is a showcase for talented craftspeople from across Ontario. Demonstrations of various crafts are featured. Crafts and home-baked goods are on sale in the Port Elgin Arena.

usually held on Wednesday during the first week of July

Kiwanis Summerfest

Forest — (519) 873-4342

Put on your dancing shoes and grab your favourite partner. This summerfest has a German flair with music, food, and lots of dancing.
usually held the first weekend in July

Annual Fireman's Carnival

Fort Erie

The candy floss, rides, and games of chance are all sponsored by Fire Company No. 1.
usually held the first weekend in July

Summer Fair

Hanover

This large agricultural fair features home-baking, crafts, and horse, pony, goat, and cattle shows.
usually held in the first weekend in July

Annual Heritage Show

Ilderton — (519) 471-8572

Recapture the past at this show of steam and gas engines, and antique cars and tractors. There's a flea market, too.
usually held the first weekend in July

Summerfest

Komoka — (519) 434-6811

This funfest features outdoor dancing, barbecues, wheelbarrow races, and a parade.

Central Canadian Fiddling and Step-Dancing Contest

Perth

Watch the experts show off their fancy fiddling and their dandy dancing.
usually held on the first weekend in July

Antique Show

Ridgetown — (519) 674-5585

This annual show and sale attracts many collectors of various collectibles.
usually held the first weekend in July

Highland Games

Cobourg

These traditional Scottish games are held at Donegan Park.
usually held the first Saturday in July

Fun Day

Fisherville — (416) 772-5489

You're sure to have fun here — a parade, arts and crafts, a horseshoe pitching tournament, a mini-tractor pull, a fish fry and a beer garden are some of the attractions that will make you smile.
usually held the first Saturday in July

Country Bluegrass Festival

Hillsburg — (519) 855-4954

Put on your stompin' boots and grab your straw hat — it's a bluegrass festival! There's square dancing, arts and crafts, and music all day and evening.
usually held the first Saturday in July

Highland Games

Brantford — (519) 756-5522

Soccer matches, a kilted golf tournament, and band concerts throughout the week lead up to the games, which are held on the last day. Pipe band and highland dance competitions, tossing the caber, and tug-of-war are some of the featured events.
usually held the second week in July

Agricultural Fair

Kingston

This fair features horse shows, livestock competitions, and grandstand entertainment.
usually held Tuesday through Saturday, the second week in July

Annual Antique Show and Sale

Lindsay

This event is held at the Victoria Park Armory.
usually held Thursday, and Friday, the second week in July

Antique Show and Sale

Madoc

This annual show and sale is held at the St. John's Anglican Church Hall.
usually held Wednesday, and Thursday of the second week in July

Muskoka Annual Arts and Crafts Show and Sale

Bracebridge — (705) 645-8255

This popular event is held at Williams Park.
usually held the second weekend in July, Friday and Saturday

Harcourt Fun Fair

Harcourt

Rides, games, and displays are featured here.
usually held the second weekend in July

Great Lakes Commercial Fisherman Convention

Port Dover — (519) 583-0918

Maybe you can pick up some fishing pointers from the experts as they combine business with pleasure. There's a tug-of-war and a fish pole competition as well as a study of commercial fishing markets and discussions on natural resources.

usually held the second weekend in July

Arts and Crafts in the Park

St. Catharines

Montebello Park is the site of this show and sale.

usually held the second weekend in July

Annual Fair and Horse Show

St. Marys — (519) 225-2130

There's lots to see and do at this agricultural fair. Events include livestock shows and competitions, fruit and vegetable displays, talent shows, and a parade.

usually held the second weekend in July

Flea Market

Teeterville — (705) 446-2557

You won't get bitten by any fleas, but you might get bitten by the flea-market-bug! Windham Township Pioneer Village is the place for bargains galore.

usually held the second weekend in July

Grand Olde Days

Wallaceburg — (519) 627-1141

You can either participate or watch the activities at this festival. It features square dancing, talent shows, a midway, and outdoor barbecues and food booths.

usually held the second weekend in July

Did you know that...

If a pair of one-pound white perch were placed in a pond, and only one percent of their offspring survived, there would be more than 2 million of them in four years.

Festival in the Park

Iroquois Falls

Take a horse and buggy ride around a park full of music, dancing, and arts and crafts.

usually held the second Sunday in July

Flying Club Air Show

Woodstock — (519) 539-2697

Watch the air show while munching on a delicious piece of barbecued chicken.

usually held the second Sunday in July

North American Banjo Contest

Durham

Get ready for some good pickin' and strummin'!

usually held in mid-July

Good Times Festival

Grimsby

Arts and crafts shows, and band concerts are just some of the events happening at the turn of the century railroad station in this town.

usually held in mid-July

Elks Millionaire Days

Keewatin

There's a carnival, games of chance, and entertainment to make you feel like a millionaire.

usually held in mid-July

Horse Show

St. Catharines

This is the largest outdoor horse show in Ontario. You'll have the chance to see all your favourite breeds.

usually held in mid-July

International Villages Festival

Brantford — (519) 753-2617

Visit "villages" of all 17 host countries and enjoy the ethnic foods, dances, music, and displays.

usually held the third week in July

River Rat Race

Oakville — (416) 845-6601

Watch the fun antics at this unique canoe race along the 26 km creek — three people per canoe, hand propulsion only!

usually held on Wednesday of the third week in July

International Week

Port Colborne — (416) 834-9765

The festivities during this week-long event include a parade, ethnic dancing, food booths, an art show, a bass derby and its logical conclusion — a fish fry!
usually held the third week in July

Gala Days

Ailsa Craig — (519) 293-3401

Don't miss the Ontario Championship Turtle Races — over 300 internationally sponsored turtles creep along in this unique event. Other feature events during Gala Days include a race for human beings, a parade, brass band concerts, and chicken and beef barbecues.
usually held on the third weekend in July

Summer Fair

Ayton

This fair features some old-time eating contests — try your hand (or stomach) at a spaghetti eating contest or a pie-eating contest! There's also a midway, horse and cattle shows, log sawing contest, races for children, and a beef barbecue.
usually held the third weekend in July

Earlton Steam and Antique Show

Earlton

Watch antique gas and steam powered cars and farm equipment come to life again. There are also displays of antiques and crafts.
usually held the third weekend in July

Agricultural Fair

Listowel — (519) 291-2850

This is a perfect chance to get away to some real country fair fun. There are many exhibits and shows of interest. Events include horse, cattle, and goat shows, a midway, farm machinery exhibits, 4-H displays, grandstand entertainment, and succulent barbecues.
usually held the third weekend in July

Summerfest

Orangeville — (519) 941-1350

There's lots of good family fun at this mid-July festival. Pancake breakfasts, log sawing, and nail driving competitions, bed races, and a farmer's market are just some of the highlights.
usually held the third weekend in July, Thursday, Friday and Saturday.

Art Show

Port Colborne — (416) 834-9765

Local talent is on display here.
usually held the third weekend in July

Antique Sale

Port Elgin

There are over 30 dealers displaying their goods at this show which is held in the Port Elgin Arena.
usually held Friday and Saturday of the third weekend in July

Rotary Threshing Festival

Thamesville — (519) 692-3991

Come see some old-time threshing machines in action at Ferguson Park.
usually held the third weekend in July

Kweshkudading Native Arts and Crafts Festival

West Bay, Manitoulin Island

Kweshkudading is an Ojibway word meaning "place where people can meet and get together." The festival involves displays and performances of the cultural arts of the native people. These arts include porcupine quill work, sweetgrass work, birchbark, leatherwork, beadwork, paintings, traditional Indian dances, and food and music.

usually held the third weekend in July

Country Good Times

Wilberforce

A three day celebration featuring a beauty contest, midway, teen dance, Western Jamboree, horse draw, and a parade.

usually held the third weekend in July

Summer Fair

Zurich — (519) 236-4511

This agricultural fair features a large horse show, a talent show, a parade, a midway, and an arm-wrestling tournament.

usually held the third weekend in July

Highland Games

Burlington — (416) 637-3744

This is a major highland event with bagpipe contests, Scottish bands, a hammer throw competition, tossing the caber, and highland dancing.

usually held the third Saturday in July

Summerfest

Exeter

Enjoy a night of dancing, music and food with a German flair.

usually held the third Saturday in July

Brant Historical Cycling Tour

Brantford — (519) 442-6235

This one-day tour takes in many of the region's historic sites. The tour leaves from Cockshutt Park. There is a registration fee.

usually held the third Sunday in July

Iroquois Summer Carnival

Iroquois — (705) 652-4889

There's a special Fly-In Breakfast for small planes (Since when do small planes eat breakfast?) plus an International Fastball Tournament.

usually held the third Sunday in July

Ethnic Festival

Timmins

There are demonstrations of arts and crafts, music, dancing and food from 11 different ethnic groups — Ukrainian, Croatian, Italian, Polish, Finnish, East Indian, Scottish, German, Romanian, Hungarian, and even Canadian people are represented at this festival.

usually held the third Sunday in July

Old Time Horseshoe Days

Gooderham — (705) 447-2039

This annual event features a midway, a talent contest, a dance, and bake sale, but the main event is a horseshoe pitching tournament.

usually held the fourth week in July

Rotary Carnival

Minden

This carnival features a parade, a midway, and displays at the fairgrounds as well as a canoe race and a footrace.

usually held the fourth week in July

Arts and Water Festival

Peterborough

A week of splashing, smashing fun! There's an arts and crafts show and sale, musical and dramatic entertainment, and many aquatic events.

usually held the last week in July

Kawartha Lakes Ontario Open Fiddle and Step-Dance Contest

Bobcaygeon

Bobcaygeon is the perfect spot for a celebration of these old-time skills.

usually held the last weekend in July

Annual Pow-Wow

Forest — (519) 873-4342

Put this in your peace-pipe and smoke it! The natives of Kettle Point Indian Reserve celebrate with traditional dances, arts and crafts, and food.

usually held the last weekend in July

Civic Quarter Horse Show

Harrow — (519) 738-6801

Participants from the U.S. and Ontario bring their favourite horses to the Harrow Arena. Try to spot the ribbon winners.

usually held the last weekend in July

Country Music Festival

Tilbury

There are festivities throughout town but the main attraction is that foot stompin' music. Country bands from all over Southwestern Ontario compete for prizes (and sheer good-times, too!)

usually held the last weekend in July

Waterloo Regional Police Association Highland Games

Cambridge — (519) 579-2211, ext. 253

Don't do anything illegal here! Events include the Canadian National Pipe Band championships, Highland dancing, tug-of-war (a chance to boo or cheer at your favourite men in blue), and a sheep-dog show.

usually held the last Saturday in July

Beef Barbecue

Drayton — (519) 638-2941

The Drayton Arena Complex is the site for this epicurean delight, sponsored by the Kinsmen.

usually held the last Saturday in July

Eastern Ontario's Firefighter's Annual Competition

Kemptville — (613) 657-4798

Not a good day for your house to catch fire!

Firefighters compete in firefighting-related contests.

usually held the last Saturday in July

Golden Horseshoe Antique Society Annual Show

Caledonia

The Caledonia Fairgrounds is the place to be for this show of antique steam equipment, antique cars, horse pulls, and arts and crafts.

usually held the end of July

Summer Fair

Delta

This agricultural fair features all kinds of farm animals in show and competition: horses, cattle, sheep, swine, and goats. There is also a midway and grandstand entertainment.

usually held at the end of July

Wikwemikong Indian Pow-Wow

South Baymouth, Manitoulin Island

Visitors are welcome at this major annual event of the Manitoulin Indians.

usually held late July/early August

Kempenfest

Barrie — (705) 726-6573

There are arts and crafts, a canoe regatta, and live theatre to please you at this country/cultural fair.

usually held the Civic Holiday Weekend

Essex County Old Time Fiddle Championship and Singing Contest

Belle River (519) 727-6366

As well as the musical events there's a pony pull, a tractor pull, and a dance.

usually held the Civic Holiday Weekend

Homecoming Weekend

Belleville

This festival has an ethnic flair, as well as beer gardens and dances.

usually held the Civic Holiday Weekend

Golden Horseshoe City

Caledonia — (416) 756-4891

This major agricultural fair has a steam-power slant as well as a horse-power one! Events include a steam rally, a Gas Era Village, a working sawmill, horse and pony pulls, a fiddle contest, and talent shows. There are also daily parades and a display of antique cars.

usually held the Civic Holiday Weekend

River Days

Chatham — (519) 352-7540

The Thames River is the centre of attention during this watery festival. Events range from water-skiing demonstrations to fireman's water hose competitions to canoe races.

usually held the Civic Holiday Weekend

Highland Games

Dutton — (519) 762-2310

You'll get a real highland welcome at the annual Dutton Games. Traditional Scottish competitions include sports, dancing, and pipe bands.

usually held the Civic Holiday Weekend

Fiddling and Step-Dancing Competition

Eganville

An old-time skills contest in the town with the famous caves.

usually held the Civic Holiday Weekend

Agricultural Fair

Lansdowne

This country fair features livestock and horse shows, farm displays, horse racing, a midway and grandstand entertainment.

usually held the Civic Holiday Weekend

The Leamington Fair

Leamington — (519) 326-4401

This agricultural fair features horse and cattle shows, a midway, and children's events.

usually held the Civic Holiday Weekend

Haliburton Rotary Carnival

Haliburton

A parade, a bed-race down the main street of Haliburton Village, plus rides, games, and a Carnival Ball all await your arrival.

usually held the Civic Holiday Weekend

Candy floss, hot dogs, caramel corn, games of chance, rides, games of skill — that's what **Lion's Club Carnivals** are all about.

Large and small communities alike hold carnivals.

Here's some of the places you'll find that carnival colour and atmosphere: **Bayfield; Dunnville (416) 774-6676; Goderich (519) 524-6635; Grimsby (416) 945-3519; Niagara Falls (416) 354-9991; Niagara-on-the-Lake; Orangeville (519) 941-4629; Port Colborne (416) 834-9765; Pt. Burwell (519) 874-4343; Seaforth (519) 527-1492; Wainfleet (416) 834-9765.**

Steam Show

Cookstown

Gas and steam engines, farm machinery, and antique cars are on display, brought to you by the Georgian Bay Steam Association.

usually held the Civic Holiday Weekend

German Festival

Dashwood

The three s's — Sausage, Sour cream, and Sauerkraut — are the mainstays of this festival. There is also a talent show, a parade, a tug-of-war, an arm-wrestling competition, and of course, lots of cold draught beer.

usually held the Civic Holiday Weekend

Summer Fair

Murillo

This agricultural fair features livestock shows plus a midway, an arts and crafts display, home baking, and chariot races.

usually held the Civic Holiday Weekend

Summer Fair

Napanee

This agricultural fair encourages spectator participation — here's a chance to discover hidden talents.

usually held the Civic Holiday Weekend

Summer Fair

Russell

There's a midway, light and heavy horse shows, and a sheep show at this agricultural fair.

usually held the Civic Holiday Weekend

Summer Jamboree

Owen Sound

The waters of Georgian Bay make a perfect backdrop for this summer celebration. Some of the attractions are a soap box derby, aquatic sports, an air show, bed races, and pancakes all day.

usually held the Civic Holiday Weekend

Calypso Weekend

Port Stanley — (519) 782-3264

This quaint fishing village comes alive with a calipso atmosphere. Stroll through an outdoor market or relax to a steel band beat in the beer gardens. There's also a boat parade and dancing.

usually held the Civic Holiday Weekend

Haweater Weekend and Indian Pow-Wow

Little Current, Manitoulin Island

What's a Haweater? Make a trip to Manitoulin Island and find out. It will be worth the trip since you can join the festivities at the beer gardens, fish fry, midway, and bicycle rodeo. There's also a Pow-Wow that features Native people from all over North America demonstrating crafts and dances.

P.S. A Haweater is one who was born on Manitoulin Island. Haw berries grow there in vast quantities.

usually held the Civic Holiday Weekend

Civic Holiday Celebrations

Oakville — (416) 845-6601

Coronation Park is still the site of this celebration, formerly known as the Mayor's Picnic. There's a pancake breakfast for early birds, and family activities throughout the day. A fireworks display is the grand finale.

usually held the Civic Holiday Weekend

Friendship Weekend

Simcoe — (519) 426-7700

It's sure to be a friendly gathering! There's art-in-the-park, beer gardens, a Festival Queen Contest, sports events, and a drum corps competition. The **Annual Antique Show and Sale**, at the Junior Farmer's Building, is also held this weekend.

usually held the Civic Holiday Weekend

Water Carnival

Temagami

This unique carnival features a regatta on Lake Temagami, dances, a grease-pole climbing contest, and water skiing competitions and displays.

usually held the Civic Holiday Weekend

Lumberjack Days

Thedford

Keep an eye out for Paul Bunyan: you'll know him when you see him — he's the tall guy with the axe!

Lumberjack events include wheelbarrow races, log rolling and cross-cutting contests, a tug-of-war, and water ball fights. There's also a barbecue and dance, and a midway.

usually held the Civic Holiday Weekend

Arts and Crafts Show

Whitby

This show and sale is held at the Arts Station Gallery.

usually held the Civic Holiday Weekend

Italian Sports Weekend

Windsor — (519) 966-2230

The biggest attraction of this event is the Ontario Tug-of-War Championships.

usually held the Civic Holiday Weekend

Downtown Carnival Mall

Blenheim

There's musical entertainment, dances, displays, and lots of bargains.

usually held the first week in August

Cobalt Miner's Festival

Cobalt — (705) 672-5579

A week of rock-breaking fun! Events include a fiddlers' contest, step-dancing, a parade, a canoe marathon, and rock-breaking!

usually held the first week of August

Gemboree

Bancroft

Are you a rockhound? Do you have trouble meeting other rockhounds? Would you like to be a rockhound? If you answer yes to one or more of the above questions, then this is the place for you. (Even if you answered no to all the questions, it will still be fun.)

The Gemboree is five days of swapping, selling, learning, and field-tripping with rocks. There is also square dancing and a carnival.

usually held in early August

Lake of the Woods International Pow-Wow

Kenora

This colourful four day event attracts native drummers and dancers from across Canada and the U.S.

usually held in early August

All that glitters is not gold

Until now, you probably thought that apetite had only to do with food and that a Muscovite was one who hailed from Moscow. However, apetite and muscovite are just 2 of 98 minerals found in the area of Bancroft, Ontario.

You'll find a wide variety of interesting rocks there. Minerals are found in almost every colour, from white to bright yellow, green, blue, purple, and black. Some are soft enough that you can scratch them with your fingernail while others are hard enough to be used for cutting and grinding. Another fascinating aspect of the different minerals is their unique crystal forms.

The first mineral collecting activity in the area was iron mining in the 1880s. Since then, a variety of commercial mining operations have gone on there including uranium mining. It has been mined there since the 1950s.

Aside from its commercial potential, Bancroft has long been a paradise for amateur rock collectors. And there's no greater evidence of that than the Bancroft Gemboree. This rock fair is held each August and attracts an estimated 25,000 visitors during its 5 day span.

Buying, selling, and swapping rocks is the primary activity at the Gemboree. Large tents are set up at the Bird's Creek grounds and about 40 rock dealers set up shop at tables inside. Outside the tents, people attending the fair who want to swap rocks set up after paying a small fee.

Other activities at the Gemboree are guided field trips to nearby areas of geological interest, lectures, and slide shows. For those who aren't just there for the rocks, there's a midway as well as other entertainment.

If you want to do some prospecting on your own, there are a number of likely sites around town. There are over 20 abandoned mines in the vicinity as well as areas where rocks are exposed because of excavations for roads or buildings. The Bancroft Chamber of Commerce provides maps of the area. It is important to get permission from the person who owns the land you're using. There's often a small fee required.

If you're captivated by the beauty of these minerals but can't see yourself digging and scratching, you may want to visit one of the jewellery stores in town. Most of them feature rocks that have been polished and set, as well as rough stones.

Alpsfest

Crystal Beach — (416) 894-2848

There is a wide variety of activities during this week-long festival: a beauty contest, a bed race, a talent show, a tug-of-war, a bathtub parade and races, an arts and crafts show and sale, and a sky-diving/parachute exhibition.

usually held the first week of August

Western Ontario Antique Show

Stratford — (519) 271-1130

Why not combine your trip to the Shakespearean Festival with a visit to this popular antique show and sale. There are over 30 outstanding dealers to choose from.

usually held the first week in August

Glengarry Highland Games

Maxville

Since its inception in 1948, the Glengarry Games have grown to be one of the largest highland events in Canada. Entrants from all over North America come to compete in pipe band, drumming, dancing, and sports competitions. Don't miss the exciting caber tossing event.

usually held the first Saturday in August

Summerfest

Minden

Enjoy the sweet sounds of jazz in the park, part of this celebration of summer.

usually held the first Saturday in August

Annual Community Picnic

Bothwell — (519) 245-3710

What an ideal mid-week family break! There are children's games, pipe bands, sports events, and a variety show at the Shetland Conservation Area.

usually held the second Wednesday in August

Annual Antique Show and Sale

Brockville

The Catholic Cultural Centre is the place to be for this visual journey into the past; you're bound to find some bargains along the way.

usually held Wednesday through Friday, the second week in August

Market Day

Huntsville

The Muskoka Pioneer Village becomes the scene of this old-time market, selling arts and crafts and antiques.

usually held the second Saturday in August

Bicycle Tour of Conestoga

Kitchener — (519) 689-6126

This tour of the Conestoga area starts at the Brenthaupt Centre. There is a registration fee.

usually held the second Sunday in August

Agricultural Fair

Dorchester

Events at this fair include livestock shows and judging, a pet show, and local entertainment.

usually held the second weekend in August

Potato Festival

Alliston

Everything you can do with a potato and more! Join in this community's celebration of the harvesting of their crop. Some of the activities include potato peeling contests, tours of potato farms, a flea market, and lots of fresh potato french fries.

usually held the second weekend in August

Agricultural Fair

Arnprior

This large agricultural fair has events such as a tractor draw, horse racing, beef and dairy cattle shows, heavy, light and western horse shows, and lamb shows.

usually held the second weekend in August

Odd Ball Olympics

Aylmer — (519) 773-3949

If you like corn-on-the-cob, this is an event you won't want to miss. All the corn-on-the-cob you can eat and corn related events such as a corn husking competition make for a good time.

usually held the second weekend in August

Agricultural Fair

Campbellford

This summer fair features cattle, horse, sheep and goat shows, craft demonstrations, a bake sale, and a midway.

usually held the second weekend in August

Highland Games

Fergus — (519) 846-9254

A town with a name like Fergus is sure to host successful highland games. The games feature the Canadian Caber Toss Championship as well as pipe band and drumming competitions, highland dancing, and a tug-of-war. These games have been held annually in Fergus since 1945 and draw crowds upwards of 30,000.

usually held the second weekend in August

Summerfest

Collingwood

This fair includes a dart tournament, an auction, a craft show, and children's events.

usually held the second weekend in August

The Comber Fair

Comber

The features at this agricultural fair are a pony drawing contest, a beauty pageant, a parade, a midway, horse shows, and musical entertainment in the evenings.

usually held the second weekend in August

Summer Fair

Lombardy

Get that old-time country feeling at the Lombardy Summer Fair. Events include cattle, sheep, swine, and goat shows, light and heavy horse shows, roots, vegetables and flowers, and a midway.

usually held the second weekend in August

Agricultural Fair

Kenora

This three day event includes a midway, a horseshoe pitching contest, a cow-milking contest, and a horse show.

usually held the second weekend in August

Haliburton County Fair

Minden

This country fair has craft displays, horse shows, grain and seed exhibits, a midway, and grandstand entertainment.

usually held the second weekend in August

Agricultural Fair

Navan

This fair features a parade, a pet show, cattle, horse, and sheep shows, and a wind-up dance on Saturday night.

usually held the second weekend in August

Annual Fair

Ridgetown — (519) 674-2921

Livestock shows and judging, craft displays, and entertainment are just a few of this agricultural fair's features.

usually held the second weekend in August

Summerfest

St. Marys — (519) 284-2340

St. Marys downtown shopping area becomes the site of a variety of family activities, and bargains too.

usually held the second weekend in August

Canadian Old Time Fiddlers' Contest

Shelburne — (519) 925-2830

This is the largest event of its kind in North America: you can hear the best fiddlers on the continent. There is also an **Antique Show** ((519) 925-3334) featuring over 50 dealers, during this fiddling weekend.

usually held the second weekend in August

Summer Fair

South River

For a country feeling in a country setting, be sure to catch all the events — log sawing and nail driving contests, cattle and horse shows, a midway, a flea market, and a barbecue.

usually held the second weekend in August

Agricultural Fair

Sutton West

There are various exhibits, plus horse racing, and a stage show at the Sutton West Agricultural Fair.

usually held the second weekend in August

Summer Fair

Vankleek Hill

This agricultural fair features dairy and beef cattle shows, heavy and light horse shows, and field crop competitions.

usually held the second weekend in August

A highland fling

Highland games competitions provide spectators with the best of two worlds — they combine the athletic traditions of the ancient Greeks that shaped the Olympic Games, with Scotland's own unique regional and cultural elements.

Sporting events such as wrestling, putting the stone, and throwing the hammer seem to have been derived, either directly or indirectly, from the ancient Greeks. But many of the other activities held at highland games are unique to Scotland and its highlands. Some of these events have faded into oblivion over the years while others are held all over the world, as in many of Ontario's small towns.

The first highland games were held in Scotland in 1819. Although sports, music, dancing, and craft competitions had probably been held long before that, 1819 seems to have been the first time they were combined. Music, dancing, and crafts were intended to relax the spectators and participants after the vigorous athletic struggles had ended.

However, the dance competitions were sometimes as fiercely competitive as the sporting events. There were occasions when the judges were unable to reach decisions on the winners and angry competitors demanded that the events be re-staged.

Tending sheep was a common occupation in the Scottish highlands and the games once reflected that strongly. Races for local shepherds were held on steep inclines and they often included hurdles not unlike the natural obstacles a shepherd might encounter on the job. Craft making competitions also showed the influence of the region. Prizes were awarded for the best wooden shepherd's crooks and walking sticks, as well as for the best knitted goods. Even the prizes were characteristically Scottish — bagpipes, tartan suits, and mulls for grinding tobacco into snuff, were awarded.

The most famous and exciting highland games event is undoubtedly tossing the caber. A caber is a long, heavy wooden log, not unlike a telephone pole. Different sources report conflicting weights and lengths for it so the only thing you can be sure of, is that it takes a burly Scotsman to fling it. Competitors balance the caber upright in their hands and flip it forward so that it somersaults before hitting the ground, the idea being to throw it as far as possible. In some competitions, the caber is so heavy that no one can make it somersault; so portions are lopped off the end until it is light enough.

One of the most prominent Scottish cultural fixtures at highland games is bagpipes. But strangely enough, they once took a back seat to the harp as Scotland's most celebrated musical instrument. However, the harp was common to Scotland and Ireland so early in the 18th century, the proud Scots adopted the pipes as their own.

Summer Fair

Williamstown

Many aspects of country fairs are rolled into one at the Williamstown Fair: there are english and harness horse shows, cattle shows, arts and crafts, and highland dancing.

usually held the second weekend in August

Peach Festival

Niagara-on-the-Lake — (416) 561-4142

You'll have a peach of a time here! There are farm tours, picnics, ethnic dancers, a peach pie baking contest, a bake sale, and lots and lots of peaches for sale.

usually held the first two weeks in August

St. Stephen's Day Celebration

Preston — (519) 745-2531

The Hungarian-Canadian Club sponsors this festival of singing, dancing, and performing groups. There is also a parade, and a dinner and dance.

usually held in mid-August

Antique Car Rally

Stouffville

Car enthusiasts from across Canada get together for this special event.

usually held in mid-August

Homecoming Week

Bancroft

Equestrian events, canoe races, horseshoe pitching and firefighting contests, log sawing and log rolling are all part of being home.

usually held the third week of August

Agricultural Fair

Barrie

There are many events at this large country fair to please old and young alike — cattle shows, horse shows, poultry shows, crafts, entertainment, food booths, and a midway.

usually held Tuesday through Sunday, the third week in August

Central Canada Exhibition

Ottawa

This large agricultural fair features a wide assortment of events. These events include horse shows, livestock judging, commercial exhibits, crafts, and grandstand shows.

usually held the third week in August

The Woodstock Fair

Woodstock

You'll find horse, cattle, goat, poultry and swine shows, a tug-of-war, crafts, and entertainment at this annual fair.

usually held the third week (fourth weekend incl.) in August

Summer Fair

Apsley

This old fashioned country fair features horse shows, children's exhibits, displays of flowers, vegetables and home baking, and a midway.

usually held the third weekend in August

The Agricultural Fair

Aylmer — (519) 773-5345

This major agricultural fair features horse and cattle shows, farm exhibits, and a midway.

usually held the third weekend in August

Antique Show

Blenheim — (519) 676-5477

Browse or buy at this annual show and sale.

usually held the third weekend in August

Western Ontario Steam Threshers Reunion

Brigden — (519) 864-1334

Come and see the machinery and men of the steam engine era.

usually held the third weekend in August

Agricultural Fair

Dunchurch

This fair has rides, exhibits, horse and cattle shows, and a Saturday night square dance.

usually held Friday and Saturday, the third weekend in August

Summer Fair

Elmira — (519) 669-8035

This is a large fair, yet it still retains a special country charm and atmosphere. There's a giant midway, horse, cattle, sheep and swine shows, 4-H competitions and exhibits, a parade of the livestock winners, crafts, and grandstand shows.

usually held the third weekend in August

The Emo Fair

Emo

This major agricultural event features livestock shows, baking and canning displays, craft shows, a log rolling contest, grandstand entertainment, and a midway.

usually held Friday and Saturday, the third weekend in August

Summer Fair

Fenelon Falls

This agricultural fair features light and heavy horse shows, calf shows, and a midway.

usually held the third weekend in August

Flower and Vegetable Show

Gravenhurst

See all your favourite horticultural varieties, and ones you didn't know existed, at this annual show, held in the Opera House.

usually held the third weekend in August

Cornfest

Mitchell — (519) 348-8429

All the corn related activities plus a parade, barbecue, and dance.

usually held Friday and Saturday, the third weekend in August

Cornfest and Summerfest

Hanover — (519) 364-4180

There's everything to do with corn plus more — a watermelon eating contest, a fishing derby, beer gardens, and a midway. There is also a band tatoo and a parade.

usually held the third weekend through the fourth, in August

Summer Folk Festival

Owen Sound

This is the 'Mariposa of the North.' Enjoy folk, bluegrass and country music on the shores of the Georgian Bay. There are three stage areas plus a children's program, and an arts and crafts area. Camping is available; tickets can be purchased in advance or at the door. Children under 12, with an adult, are admitted free.

usually held the third weekend in August

Fun Fair

Lucan (519) 227-4221

In a land of leprechauns and four-leaf clovers, this fair is bound to bring you good luck! There's good country music, Irish music, horse shows, craft displays, and a midway.

usually held the third weekend in August

Ottawa Valley Steam and Antique Show

Petawawa

See all kinds of steam powered machinery — there are tractors and threshing machines, steam driven butter churns, and even steam powered washing machines. There are also vintage gas and diesel cars on display.

usually held the third weekend in August

Agricultural Fair

Merrickville

Merrickville offers an assortment of country fair festivities — there's a parade, livestock judging, horse shows, antique and weaving displays, plus an antique car and steam show.

usually held the third weekend in August

Agricultural Fair

North Shore

If you missed sugaring-off this spring, be sure to catch the maple sugar demonstrations featured at this fair. There are also pony, chariot and chuck wagon races, horse and cattle shows, and a beef barbecue.

usually held the third weekend in August

Arts and Crafts Weekend

Harrow — (519) 738-2029

The John Richardson Park Homestead, Iler Road and County Road 50, is the site of this annual show and sale.

usually held the third weekend in August

Agricultural Fair

Peterborough

Featured at this country fair are horse and cattle shows, grandstand shows, and crafts.

usually held the third weekend in August

Agricultural Fair

South Mountain

South Mountain's fair has English, western, and heavy horse shows, sheep and goat shows, and agricultural exhibits.

usually held the third weekend in August

Fall Fair

Providence Bay

Help celebrate the harvest with this community. Events include flower, grain, fruit and vegetable exhibits, a bake sale, needlecraft displays, and country and western entertainment.

usually held the third weekend in August

Agricultural Fair

Stirling

This fair features horse racing, a tractor pull, cattle, goat, and horse shows, agricultural exhibits, crafts, and grandstand shows.

usually held the third weekend in August

Fall Fair

Strathroy — (519) 245-3944

This annual agricultural fair features a midway, livestock exhibits, grandstand entertainment, and a dance.

usually held the third weekend in August

Annual Flower and Vegetable Show

Callander

All the fragrances and colours of summer will be on display here.

usually held the third Saturday in August

Agricultural Fair

Parham

This one-day country event features a Pie Queen Contest, a midway, livestock exhibits, and craft displays.

usually held the third Saturday in August

Summerfest

Port Dover

An arts and crafts show and sale, an auction of antiques, and a dance in the evening make this a fun summer day.

usually held the third Saturday in August

Summer Fair

Avonmore

This agricultural fair has horse and cattle shows, horse races, and an exhibition of baking, sewing, vegetables, and cheese

usually held the third Sunday in August

Ravenswood Arts and Crafts Sale

Ravenswood

Many different crafts are represented at this show and sale.

usually held the third Sunday in August

Agricultural Fair

Blackstock

Events at this fair include a parade, a midway, livestock and horse show, a frog jumping contest, a spaghetti eating contest, a cow-milking contest, and a horseshoe pitching tournament.

usually held Friday and Saturday, the fourth weekend in August

Agricultural Fair

Bonfield

Attractions at this country fair include horse shows, craft displays, a midway, a cattle show, western games, and a sea-pie and bean supper.

usually held the fourth weekend in August

Fall Fair

Chesterville

This large agricultural fair features a western horse show, horse races, sheep and cattle shows, crafts, beer gardens, and a dance.

usually held the fourth weekend in August

Fall Fair

Cobden

This agricultural fair features horse, cattle, sheep, goat, and pet shows, a 4-H show, and nightly entertainment.

usually held the fourth weekend in August, Thursday to Saturday

Old Time Fiddlers' Contest and Jamboree

Drayton — (519) 638-2190

At the Drayton Arena, this fiddling contest will get your feet moving!

usually held the fourth weekend in August

Fall Fair

Dresden — (519) 683-2429

At this major agricultural fair you'll find a Fair Queen Contest, a midway, a stage show, a tractor pull, livestock, grain and horticultural exhibits and competitions, machinery demonstrations, crafts, and home baking.

usually held the fourth weekend in August, Thursday to Saturday

Rural Corn Festival

Kitchener — (519) 744-5382

There's lots of corn-on-the-cob and home baking at this festival, held at the Doon Pioneer Village.

usually held the fourth weekend in August

Fall Fair

Dryden

This agricultural fair has a little bit of everything. There's livestock and horse shows, displays of agricultural products and field crops, crafts, baking, canning, sewing, a midway, and square dancing.

usually held Thursday, Friday and Saturday, the fourth weekend in August

Agricultural Fair

Cochrane

Some of the features here are horse and cattle shows, baking and canning exhibits, vegetable displays, flower shows, and a midway.

usually held Friday and Saturday, the fourth weekend in August

Downtown Country Fair Days

Listowel

The downtown area becomes the site of bargains, a midway, and country displays.

usually held the fourth weekend in August

Fall Fair and Craft Show

Markdale

This country fair boasts livestock and horse shows, a beef barbecue and dance, talent shows, plus a large craft show.

usually held the fourth weekend in August

Agricultural Fair

Massey

This four-day fair has grown over the last seventy years to include a midway, a parade, and grandstand show. But it hasn't lost the old time agricultural exhibits and horse shows.

usually held the fourth weekend in August

Fall Fair

Odessa

This agricultural fair features English and western horse shows, a large poultry show, a parade, a talent show and a beer tent.

usually held the fourth weekend in August, Friday and Saturday

Fall Fair

Porquis

At this country fair you'll find livestock and horse shows, plus exhibits. This fair has been held annually for over 60 years.

usually held Friday and Saturday, the fourth weekend in August

Antique Car Rally and Craft Show

Port Rowan

Backus Conservation Area is the site for this gathering of car and/or craft enthusiasts.

usually held the fourth weekend in August

Antique Show and Sale

Sarnia

Why not start your Christmas shopping early? The Sarnia Holiday Inn hosts this annual show and sale.

usually held the fourth weekend in August

Annual Fair and Tractor Pull

Shedden — (519) 764-2939

As well as its headline event, there are horse and cattle shows, horse races, a safety rodeo by Junior Farmers, and craft displays.

usually held the fourth weekend in August, Friday and Saturday

Annual Turkey Festival

Strathroy — (519) 245-1070

You'll be "talking-turkey" when you leave this fun filled three day festival! There's a midway, hot-air balloon rides, a parade, grandstand shows, and an antique automobile display. Turkey events include turkey races, turkey bingo, roast turkey dinner, and a variety of turkey recipes. Gobble—gobble—gobble!

usually held the fourth weekend in August

Cornfest

Tecumseh — (519) 735-2184

There's band entertainment, a giant parade on Saturday, and some "corny" activities at this annual festival.

usually held the fourth weekend in August

Tri-County Fair

Tillsonburg — (519) 877-2957

This large agricultural fair draws participants from three counties. There are horse shows, agricultural and commercial displays, livestock shows, as well as grandstand entertainment, and a fiddlers' contest.

usually held the fourth weekend through the last week in August

Talking turkey

Labelling someone a turkey may be a more vicious remark than you intended. These hapless birds are renowned for their stupidity, particularly when they're young. When young turkeys (poults) are first put in a heated brooder house, the farmer must surround the brooder stove with a circular cardboard "fence." This prevents the poults from piling up in the corners of the room so much that they smother each other.

Poults are not exactly fussy eaters either. They will try to eat almost anything small enough to put in their beaks. Because of this, farmers must be careful not to leave such delicacies such as straw, wood shavings, or coarse sawdust within gobbling distance. This kind of debris is usually covered by burlap or sacking. The poults' lack of intelligence is complemented by their lack of agility. If the debris is covered with paper, it is too slippery for them and will cause leg injuries.

Fall Fair

Thedford — (519) 296-4243

There are lots of contests to show off your skills at this agricultural fair — how about a freckle contest, or a balloon-blowing contest, or a cross-cut sawing contest, or a horseshoe pitching contest, or maybe pie-eating is your forte? There are also horse shows, agricultural exhibits, a midway, and a dance.

usually held the fourth weekend in August

Fall Fair

Trout Creek

This agricultural fair features livestock and horse shows, arts and crafts shows, home baking, and a midway.

usually held the fourth weekend in August, Friday and Saturday

Fall Fair

Denbigh

Log loading and a horse draw are just two of the scheduled events at this agricultural fair.

usually held the fourth Saturday in August

Fall Fair

Coe Hill

There is something for all the family here — livestock and horse shows, 4-H Club exhibits, a western show, a talent show, and a midway.

usually held the fourth Saturday in August

Annual Flower and Vegetable Show

North Bay

See all your favourite varieties here.

usually held the fourth Sunday in August

Peach Festival

Winona — (416) 643-3214

You're sure to have a peachy-keen time! There's a stamp show and sale, a bed race, arts and crafts displays, a midway, helicopter rides, food booths, and a Peach Queen Contest.

usually held the fourth weekend in August

Fall Fair

Maberly

This fair has all the old time country favourites — 4-H club displays, horse shows, maple syrup demonstrations, hand made quilt displays, home baking and pickle displays, and a home cooked turkey supper.

usually held the fourth Saturday in August

Summerfest

Port Elgin — (519) 832-2761

This community celebrates summer with music, dancing, and good food.

usually held the fourth Saturday in August

Fall Fair

Rosseau

This fair offers log sawing contests, nail driving contests, races, and square dancing.

usually held the fourth Saturday in August

Bean Festival

Zurich — (519) 236-4974

The "best home cooked beans in the world" are the focus of attention at this annual event. The main street of this village is blocked off to form a mall featuring a street market, a midway and entertainment. There's a wide variety of activities, including the Canadian Horseshoe Championships.

usually held the fourth Saturday in August

Highland Games

Parry Sound

These games have all the Scottish pageantry you could imagine — pipe bands, tossing the caber, and highland dancing.

usually held in late-August

Early Ontario Architecture

Small towns are excellent places to look for examples of old Ontario architecture. The towns with the oldest buildings are often situated near water. Some of the best areas to look are along the north shore of the St. Lawrence, around Lake Ontario, the Niagara Peninsula, and around Lake Erie. Other good spots are along rivers such as the Ottawa, the Rideau, the Thames, the Speed, and the Grand.

The characteristics of architectural styles are often quite well defined. For example, many styles have a fixed number of panes of glass in each window. Other characteristics relate to shape, roof style, and ornate details or the lack of them.

You won't need to read an article to identify Ontario's first type of dwelling. The settler's log cabin is probably the best known example of early architecture. The only trouble you might have is in distinguishing pioneer cabins from those built by modern day back-to-the-landers. The earliest settler's cabins have fireplaces, which were used for cooking and heating. Later pioneer cabins had iron stoves for the same purposes. The cabins usually had 1 or 2 rooms on the main floor and sometimes a loft for sleeping. The best place to find settler's cabins is in the northern parts of Ontario.

Georgian homes are considerably scarcer than log cabins. They were built between the years 1783 and 1810. Some characteristics associated with them were rectangular shape, steep roofs, tight eaves, square or round headed front door openings, simple mouldings, casement or double hung sashes with 24 panes, heavy doors with 6 panels, and plain mantels with bold shelves above them.

Some significant changes were made between the Georgian style and the Loyalist style. Loyalist homes were built between 1800 and 1835 and they featured great detail on a small scale. Their characteristics included a multiplicity of small mouldings, thin 6 or 8 panel doors, elliptical arches over front doors with side lights, gentler sloping pitched roofs, 20 or 24 pane sashes, and elegant mantels.

Another style which became popular in public buildings and larger homes was the Italianate style. These elegant buildings were built between 1845 and 1870. Highlights of this style included a tower, groups of round headed windows, tall and graceful French doors and windows, verandahs and balconies with high ceilings, and gently sloping roofs with wide overhangs.

The dominant style in many Ontario buildings from the nineteenth century is the Gothic Revival style. And one of the best examples of it is Ottawa's Parliament Buildings, first constructed in 1866 and rebuilt after the fire of 1916. Most buildings of this type were built between 1835 and 1890. Many of them feature both Greek and Gothic details.

Travel notes

Fall

Although the autumn marks a beginning for teachers and students, it marks the end of a hard working-year for farmers. The crops have been sown, nurtured, and reaped, the pickles and jams have been made, and the pantry is stocked for the long winter ahead. It's the perfect time for agricultural fairs.

Fall fairs provide farmers with the opportunity to show the fruits of their labours. Most of these fairs include horse shows, tractor pulls, cooking and pickling contests, livestock competitions, and educational exhibits.

Part of the fun of attending a fall fair is the trip itself. Much of the country in Ontario is forested and the coloured leaves alone make the trip worthwhile.

The fall is an excellent time to begin your Christmas shopping. You're bound to find some unique items at the many fall craft fairs and auctions.

Fall Fair

Bayfield — (519) 565-2126

At this agricultural fair you'll find lots of interesting things: old time farm machinery, crafts, a poultry show, a horse show, vegetables, fruits and flowers, a log sawing contest, and a tug-of-war.

usually held Labour Day weekend, Friday and Saturday

Fall Fair

Beachburg

At this fair you'll find craft displays, horse shows, beef and dairy cattle shows, horticultural shows, and a midway.

usually held Labour Day weekend, Friday through Sunday

Fall Fair

Burk's Falls

Enjoy a breath of fresh country air in Burk's Falls. Their agricultural fair includes a log sawing contest, a fiddlers' contest, agricultural displays and exhibits, a gymnastics performance, and a midway.

usually held Labour Day Weekend

Cayugafest

Cayuga — (416) 772-5708

Join in this community's farewell to summer. Activities include a teen dance, a beer garden, a tractor pull, a beef barbecue, canoe races, a stilt race, and a water ski show.

usually held Labour Day weekend

Fall Fair

Centreville

Events at this agricultural fair include a baby show, horse races, school exhibits, and crafts.

usually held Labour Day weekend, Friday and Saturday

Agricultural Fair

Charlton

This country fair features over 40 competitions in cattle, horses, sheep, vegetables, and grains. See the biggest and the best of everything.

usually held Labour Day weekend, Friday and Saturday

Fall Fair

Coldwater and District

The village of Coldwater hosts this agricultural fair which features western and pony shows, harness racing, and a parade.

usually held Thursday through Sunday, Labour Day weekend

Great Northern Exhibition

Collingwood

There's an old time fiddlers' contest, craft displays, light and heavy horse shows, sheep and cattle shows, a hog auction, pony pulls, and a midway. And there's good home baking to satisfy even the greatest hunger.

usually held Labour Day weekend

Cycling Tour of Elora and Mennonite Country

Elora — (519) 442-6235

It's hard to find prettier country, and a bicycle seat offers an excellent vantage point!

usually held Labour Day weekend

Fall Fair

Foley (Twp. in Parry Sound County)

Enjoy a beef barbecue after a day's country activities. Horse shows, and agricultural exhibits are held during the day.

usually held Labour Day weekend, Friday through Sunday

Fall Fair

Harrow — (519) 738-6801

This country fair has been drawing crowds for over 125 years! With so much to offer, it's easy to see why. There's grandstand entertainment each evening, craft displays, 4-H exhibits, a pony pulling match, horse shows, cattle, sheep, swine, and poultry shows, displays of field and garden produce, plus a midway.

usually held Labour Day weekend

Fall Fair

Hymers

There are races and contests for the whole family — why not try your luck? There are also horse shows, old time fiddlers, and pipe bands.

usually held Sunday and Monday, Labour Day weekend

Fall Fair

Kincardine

Let this be your grande finale to the summer. There are horse and livestock shows, a tug-of-war, and a Queen of the Fair Contest.

usually held Labour Day weekend

Fall Fair

Kinmount

This agricultural fair features livestock and horse shows, steam engine exhibits, craft displays, and a midway.

usually held Labour Day weekend

Romanian Cultural Festival

Kitchener — (519) 743-6095

Sports and dance competitions, and music will keep you entertained at Bingeman Park.

usually held Saturday and Sunday, Labour Day weekend

Central Ontario Exhibition

Kitchener — (519) 885-7123

This is one of the largest agricultural fairs. It is held at the Kitchener Auditorium and features agricultural, industrial, and service exhibitions, cattle, horse and poultry shows, a midway, beer gardens, and nightly enterment.
usually held Labour Day weekend

Fall Fair

Magnetawan

This fall fair has been going strong for over 100 years! Attractions include livestock and horse shows, craft and antique displays, log sawing and horseshoe pitching contests, and square dancing.
usually held Labour Day weekend

Fall Fair

Marmora

Bid farewell to summer in a country setting — cattle, horse, and goat shows, and crafts help ease the parting pains.
usually held Labour Day weekend, Saturday through Monday

Fall Fair

Matheson

Try your luck at one of the old-time contests to be found here — choose from a Meadow Muffin Throwing Contest, or a Watermelon Spitting Contest! Other events include a Harvest Queen Contest, agricultural exhibits, a parade with pipe bands, local talent show, and an antique auction.
usually held Labour Day weekend, Saturday and Sunday

Country fairs

Agricultural fairs in Ontario have always been good places to combine business with pleasure. Fairs began in the early 1800s as occasions for buying, trading, and selling. They also provided farmers with the opportunity to sound each other out on topics such as seeds and crops, breeding farm animals, and the latest developments in farm implements and machinery.

Fair organizers began to award prizes for various farm achievements. Some of the prizes were given for general achievements over a long period of time, such as best and longest serving farmhand, or best managed farm. Other prizes of a more specific nature were given for quality and yield of crops per acre, and livestock. Some typical categories and prizes were $5 for the best cow, $2 for the best cheese, and $1.50 for best maple syrup.

Fairs were not only a chance to recognize the achievements of peers; they gradually came to fill more of a social function. Some of the activities held included horse races, banquets, dances, physical contests, and ploughing matches.

Farmers were generally hard-working people, and the fairs were one of the few opportunities they got to let off some steam. Sometimes they were quite lively. Ottawa's first public fair in 1829 was a case in point. It seems that lots of drinking went on in some of the tents set up at the fair. Late in the day, an alcohol-fueled brawl broke out at the horse races. The incident caused quite a stir and it was several years before another fair was held there.

As the social aspect of the fairs developed, there was some criticism of the direction they were going in. Some people suggested that the fairs were deviating from what they were intended to be — serious agricultural events. Some of the fun events were looked upon as too frivolous or insulting to the intelligence of the farming community.

Happily enough, today fairs seem to strike a good balance between agriculture and recreation. You'll still find ploughing matches and livestock judging but you'll also find midways, sporting events, beauty pageants, and talent shows.

Fall Fair

Melbourne — (519) 289-5772

This small community holds a fall fair thats big on fun! Events include horse races, livestock shows, arts and crafts displays, a parade, and a midway.

usually held Labour Day weekend

Steam Era

Milton

There's so much to see at this fair, you'll hardly know where to begin — but don't let that stop you! There are displays and demonstrations of steam engines, threshing machines, and tractors; log sawing and sheath tying contests; arts and crafts displays; and grandstand entertainment. The **Annual Antique Show and Sale** ((416) 325-1820) is also held at this time.

usually held Labour Day weekend

Fall Fair

Mitchell — (519) 348-8429

Billed as "the biggest little fair in Ontario", the Mitchell Fall Fair features country handicrafts, baked goods, cattle, swine and horse shows, plus many special events.

usually held Labour Day weekend

Fall Fair

Newington (Stormont)

At this agricultural fair you'll find a parade, dairy cattle shows, heavy and light horse shows, a tractor rodeo, and a barbecue.

usually held Labour Day weekend

Mardi-Gras

Port Elgin

A street carnival, barbecue and dance create a grande finale to summer.

usually held Labour Day weekend

Rare hair

As you admire the shining coats of the horses at agricultural fairs, keep in mind that their gleaming beauty has a few practical uses.

Horsehair once had many uses around the home. In the 19th century, it was a popular upholstery material and the horsehair couch was a common piece of living room furniture. The horsehair fabric covering the sofa was actually a blend; this stiff open weave material usually had a cotton warp and a horsehair weft. Horsehair was also used for furniture and mattress stuffing. Usually the un-spun, short hairs were used for this.

Not many pieces of furniture are stuffed with horsehair today and even fewer are covered with it. However, horsehair is still used today in other ways. Bristle brushes, paintbrushes, and other brushes for personal and industrial uses are often made with it. One of its most specialized uses is for the strings of violin bows. The material used for that is the long, high grade, white horse hair from the animal's tail.

Agricultural Fair

New Liskeard

You'll find lots of country things here — horse shows, dairy and beef cattle shows, 4-H exhibitions, and a parade.

usually held Labour Day weekend

Cereal Harvesting

Oakville — (416) 827-6911

See the harvesting and threshing of cereal grains with horse and steam powered equipment. It all happens at the Bronte Creek Provincial Park.

usually held Labour Day weekend

Fall Fair

Orangeville — (519) 941-1490

Events at this agricultural fair include farm exhibits, steer, sheep, and swine shows, and track and field events.

usually held Labour Day weekend

Fall Fair

Paris — (519) 632-7590

You'll find many attractions at this large agricultural fair. Choose from events such as horse shows, tractor pulls, horse races, livestock exhibitions, an antique car rally, and a midway.

usually held Labour Day weekend

Upper Ottawa Valley Fiddling and Step-dancing Contest and Fall Fair

Pembroke

Two favourite country pastimes are highlighted here — plus all the exhibitions and shows usually found at agricultural fairs.

usually held Labour Day weekend

Fall Fair

Perth

Bid the summer farewell at this country fair. Events include cattle, sheep, goat, poultry and horse shows, a midway, crafts, and a parade.
usually held Labour Day weekend

Fall Fair

Port Perry

Events at this agricultural fair include horse racing, beef and dairy cattle shows, horse shows, a miniature tractor pull, a horseshoe pitching contest, and a display of antique farm equipment.
usually held Sunday and Monday, Labour Day weekend

Agricultural Fair

Shannonville

Can you catch a greasy pig? Watch the fun as contestants try! There are also log sawing and nail driving contests, a fiddlers' contest, livestock and horse shows, and a midway.
usually held Saturday and Sunday, Labour Day weekend

Agricultural Fair

Riceville

There's all kinds of country fair flavour in Riceville!
usually held Labour Day weekend, Friday through Sunday

Community Days and Parade

St. Catharines

The whole town comes out for this one! The Merriton Community Park is the site of the festivities, highlighted by a midway.
usually held Labour Day weekend

Fall Fair

Smithville — (416) 957-3746

This agricultural fair features horse, cattle, and sheep shows, a log sawing contest, poultry and rabbit shows, and a midway.
usually held Labour Day weekend

Talbot Shivaree

St. Thomas

A shivaree is a noisy demonstration or celebration, a mock serenade with bottles and horns to a couple on their wedding night. There's no guarantee of newlyweds, but there's sure to be a lively time in St. Thomas. The celebrations include children's rides, music, and a street dance.
usually held on Labour Day weekend

Rockhound Fair

Wilberforce

Enjoy a rock festival without ear-splitting guitars and crazed kids! This fair features rock exhibits, swapping, field trips, and a Rockhound dance.

Fireman's Field Day Celebrations

Windsor — (519) 255-6489

This celebration includes a midway, sports competitions, entertainment, and highland games.
usually held Labour Day weekend

Pioneer Craft Day and Corn Roast

Peterborough

See your favourite crafts, and munch your favourite veg! This fair is held at Century Village.
usually held Labour Day

Corn Cob Capers

Milton — (416) 878-4131

There's nothing too mysterious about these capers. They take place in broad daylight at the Mountsberg Wildlife Centre. This pioneer corn festival features demonstrations of antique corn mulchers and apple cider presses. And lest we overlook the obvious... lots of corn-on-the-cob.
held Saturdays, Sundays, and holidays in September

Quinte Exhibition

Belleville

This is one of the larger agricultural fairs and features dairy, beef and 4-H cattle shows, sheep, swine, poultry and horse shows, crafts, home baking, and a midway.
usually held the second week in September, Tuesday through Sunday

Western Fair

London

This fair has grown to be the second largest agricultural exhibition in Canada. Events include livestock and horse shows, farm displays, and 4-H competitions. There is also a large midway and grandstand entertainment.
usually held the second week in September

Rolling pins

Rolling pins were designed to flatten out cookie and pie crust dough. Over the years the styles have altered slightly, but their function remains the same.

The earliest rolling pins had no handles; later long handles were carved as one piece with the roller. Next came rolling pins with carved handles. Some pins even had hand carved designs on the rolling part of them — these were used to produce special patterned cookies. Another pin style, known as a French rolling pin, has no handles; the ends of the pin taper off from a thick centre.

Not all pins were made of wood; glass rolling pins were very popular. Some of the glass pins had corks so that they could be filled with ice water. Any baker will tell you that cold dough is easier to work with.

Collecting old rolling pins, and other kitchen utensils, is an interesting hobby. Some of the old tools can still be used, while others are too fragile. An old wooden salad bowl, filled with various wooden utensils, adds character to any kitchen. To tell if a rolling pin is really old, check its diameter. It should be uneven due to the shrinkage of the wood.

Fall Fair

Tara

Why not take a break in mid-week, and visit a country fair? This one offers horse races, cattle and pony competitions, agricultural exhibits, and a Baking Queen Contest.
usually held Tuesday and Wednesday, the second week in September

Niagara Regional Exhibition

Welland — (416) 735-6413

This large agricultural fair offers something for everybody — grandstand entertainment, industrial, agricultural and livestock exhibits, horse, cattle and poultry shows, an old time fiddlers' and step-dancers' contest, horticultural exhibits, baking contests, and a midway.
usually held the second week, Tuesday through Sunday, in September

Fall Fair

Palmerston — (519) 343-2603

At this old time country fair you'll find light, heavy, hunter and jumper horse shows, western games, crafts and a midway.
usually held Wednesday and Thursday, the second week of September

Fall Fair

Sunderland

Get away to clean country air, in the middle of the week? Why not? You'll find all the excuses you'll need here — horse races, pony games, agricultural exhibits, 4-H competitions, and a Fair Queen Contest.
usually held Wednesday, the second week in September

Fall Fair

Wellesley — (519) 656-2089

Another spot for that mid-week retreat is this agricultural fair in Wellesley. All the animals — horses, sheep, cattle, swine — will be there; lots of contests — tug-of-war, bed races, talent show — will be going on; plus lots of other activities — midway, sheep shearing, and spinning and weaving demonstrations. Plan to take that well-deserved break!

usually held Tuesday and Wednesday, the second week in September

Fall Fair

Acton

Acton's fall fair features horse, cattle and poultry shows, a horse pull, a tractor pull, a fiddlers' contest, and a midway.

usually held the second weekend in September

Fall Fair

Almonte

You'll see exotic breeds of cattle, horses, and sheep, farm machinery, and local talent. There are home cooked meals available, and a midway.

usually held the second weekend in September, Thursday to Saturday

Fall Fair

Arthur — (519) 848-5201

All kinds of country activities await you here. There are cattle, horse, sheep, and swine shows, flower shows, arts and crafts displays, home baking, and a midway.

usually held the second weekend in September

Lincoln County Fair

Beamsville — (416) 563-7071

Just what the doctor ordered — country fun in country air! There's a midway, agricultural exhibits, livestock, poultry and horse shows, harness racing, pony racing, and a talent show.

usually held the second weekend in September

Fall Fair

Beaverton

At this agricultural fair you'll find light and heavy horse shows, a pigeon show, the 4-H County Championship show, and a midway.

usually held Friday and Saturday, the second weekend in September

Fall Fair

Beaver Valley (dispersed rural community in Artemesia Twp., Grey Cty.)

Country events here include a Fair Queen Contest, Fiddlers' Contest, horse and calf competitions, and crafts.

usually held the second weekend in September, Friday and Saturday

Fall Fair

Binbrook — (416) 692-4418

Celebrate the harvest with this community. Festivities include horse, sheep, poultry and cattle shows, crafts, home baking, and a midway.

usually held the second weekend in September

Huron Pioneer Steam Threshers Reunion

Blyth — (613) 523-9278

Get involved in these three days of action and nostalgia. Antique steam engines, talent shows, parade and dances will take you back in time. The reunion is held at the Agricultural Park.

usually held the second weekend in September

Fall Fair

Bracebridge

This fair combines the colours of the season with the joys of country living to produce a bright, happy fair. Events include poultry, cattle, horse and pony shows, a horseshoe pitching contest, arts and crafts displays, and vegetable shows.

usually held the second weekend in September

Fall Fair

Brampton

This agricultural fair captures the essence of country fairs. There are competitions in canning, baking, square dancing, needlework, crafts, fruits, flowers and vegetables. There are light harness and heavy horse shows, cattle shows, an antique car show, and a pet show.

usually held the second weekend in September

Agricultural Fair

Caledon

Arrive in time for the parade on Saturday afternoon. The rest of the day, enjoy horse and livestock shows, 4-H club exhibits, and talent shows. Why not enter some of the family contests?

usually held Friday and Saturday, the second weekend in September

Agricultural Fair

Cambridge (Galt)

All your favourite animals are here — sheep, goats, swine, horses, and cattle. There's also a midway and grandstand entertainment.

Cambridge also holds their **Annual Antique Show and Sale** this weekend, at the arena.

usually held the second weekend in September

Bruce Mines Exhibition

Bruce Mines

This old time agricultural fair has a bit of everything. There are horse, rabbit, sheep, goat, swine, poultry and cattle shows, vegetable, grain, and fruit shows, crafts, and a farm machinery display.

usually held the second weekend in September

Fall Fair

Chesley

Country fair activities here include horse, pony and cattle shows, agricultural exhibits, craft displays, and a midway.

usually held Friday and Saturday, the second weekend in September

Agricultural Fair

Clarence Creek

This fair features a midway, horse shows, and a dance.

usually held the second weekend in September

Fall Fair

Cookstown

There's lots cookin' in Cookstown this fall fair weekend!

usually held the second weekend in September

Tobacco Harvest Festival

Delhi — (519) 582-3911

Smoking and tobacco can sometimes cause conflicts in restaurants, line-ups and other public places, but there won't be any conflicts here — just good ol' fun! (And nobody will make you smoke!) Some of the events are a tug-of-war, a fireworks display, and a Harvest Queen Contest. Also, there's a beer garden, ethnic entertainment and dancing.

usually held the second weekend in September

Fall Fair

Desboro

There are 4-H Club competitions, horseshoe pitching contests, baking and canning displays, arts and crafts, and a field crop competition at the Desboro Fall Fair.

usually held Friday and Saturday, the second weekend in September

Fall Fair

Drayton — (519) 638-3185

The Drayton Arena and Fairgrounds is the site of horse and sheep shows, homecrafts, baking, and a midway.

usually held the second weekend in September

Fall Fair

Dundalk

It's harvest time, and what could be a better way to celebrate than a country fair? Dundalk's features cattle, horse and goat shows, pony races, displays of field and garden produce, arts and crafts, home cooking, and a midway.

usually held the second weekend in September, Friday and Saturday

Timber lines

Move over and make room for Ontario's trees. Only 9 percent of Ontario's land area is not classified as forested.

Before deciding that trees are villains for crowding us out, keep in mind that 75,000 people in Ontario are directly employed in forest product industries. And thousands more are working in areas indirectly related to forestry.

Think for a moment of all the wood and paper products we use, which are beneficial aspects of forestry we don't often think of. Many products that one doesn't usually associate with trees contain wood or wood by-products. Some examples of such products are film, coal, plastics, adhesives, and even some drugs.

Forestry is also important in that it provided the impetus for developing many remote areas of Ontario. There are a handful of small towns that depend heavily on forestry. Roads that were built to gain access to forests have also opened up wilderness areas for recreational use.

Trees also provide residents of Ontario with some of their most popular agricultural products. Most of the fruit growth in the Niagara region comes from trees. And though it doesn't exactly grow on trees, maple syrup is certainly a favourite treat.

Trees are also part of a complex ecosystem and they play some important roles in maintaining it. Their functions include, manufacturing some of our oxygen, providing shelter for important wildlife species, and preventing excessive soil erosion by catching rainfall in their boughs.

Raising Christmas trees is a surprisingly lucrative branch of forestry. Trees are sold for export to the United States, the Caribbean, and South America as well as to domestic markets. More than 2 million trees are exported each year, providing revenue of almost 4 million dollars.

Not all the beneficial aspects of trees can be measured in such concrete terms. Consider the psychological lift that the colour of leaves in the fall gives our failing spirits. Without the brilliant colours, autumn would certainly be drab. And although nobody has measured out how many cubic feet of shade trees in Ontario provide, they are of utmost importance on hot, sunny days. The final point to be mentioned in praise of trees is a patriotic one. Without the maple leaf, what would Canada do for a flag?

Arts and Crafts Show and Sale

Elliot Lake

This annual event has a variety of work by many talented people.
usually held the second weekend in September

Fall Fair

Embro

There is a unique collection of Scottish exhibits at this agricultural fair as well as horse, cattle and sheep shows, and grandstand entertainment.
usually held the second weekend in September

Fall Fair

Englehart

Features at this agricultural fair are a quilt exhibit, horse shows, a cattle show, a flower show, and a baby contest.
usually held the second weekend in September, Thursday through Saturday

Fall Fair

Feversham

At this fair you'll find log sawing, nail driving, and bubble gum chewing(?) contests, a pet show, horse shows, flowers, and baking.
usually held Friday and Saturday, the second weekend in September

Fall Fair

Florence — (519) 692-5168

Florence's fall fair features, besides alliteration, a children's pet and hobby parade, an antique automobile and engines show, 4-H livestock shows, and the best baked breads.
usually held the second weekend in September

Fall Fair

Fergus — (519) 843-1712

If you enjoyed this town's hospitality during their Highland Games, here's another chance to capture some warmth and good country feelings. This agricultural fair features a horse pull, a saddle horse show, a field crop competition, an art show, and a midway.
usually held the second weekend in September

Antique Sale and Show

Green Valley

Nostalgia, collectibles and some rare items can be found at this annual event, held at the Green Valley Pavilion.
usually held the second weekend in September

Fall Fair

Lakefield

Watch your movements during the auctioneer's competition! Otherwise you might walk away with a lighter wallet and a can of striped paint or a fully automatic antique pretzelbender! Some less risky events to enjoy at this Fall Fair are the horse, cattle, and goat shows and 4-H exhibits.
usually held the second weekend in September

Fall Fair

Lucknow

You'll have luck now, when you're in Lucknow for their fall fair. There are tug-of-war, log sawing and pole climbing contests, and wheelbarrow races, as well as horse, cattle, and goat shows, a midway, and variety entertainment.
usually held Friday and Saturday the second weekend in September

Fruit fools

These fools are not silly at all. They're sweet, light and delightful to eat. But they're so easy to make, even a fool can manage.

Fools are basically pureed fruit and whipped cream. Almost any fruit can be made into a fool; most require no cooking. Fruit purees can be sweetened with sugar, or liqueurs. All you do is fold the puree into whipped cream — presto a fool!

Some fruits require cooking and sweetening. Gooseberries are one, but the extra effort is worth it.

Gooseberry Fool

You'll need one quart of fresh, ripe gooseberries (about 5 cups), about 1 cup white sugar, and 2 cups heavy cream. Begin by topping and tailing the gooseberries. Place them in a saucepan with a bit of water, and cook and mash them over low heat for about 30 minutes. Add the sugar and simmer until it dissolves. Taste the mixture and add more sugar if your sweet tooth is not yet satisfied. Press the mixture through a sieve to remove the seeds, and chill it. When the gooseberry puree is completely chilled, whip the cream. Fold the fruit into the cream, leaving pretty swirls. Scoop into parfait glasses.

Serve the fool to four of your favourite fools.

Fall Fair

Manitowaning

There's a bake sale, crafts, entertainment, and livestock judging at this country fair.
usually held Friday and Saturday, the second weekend in September

Antique Exhibition and Sale

Markham

You're sure to find that special gift or treasure at this annual show and sale, held at the Markham Arena.
usually held the second weekend in September

Fall Fair

Meaford and St. Vincent

This country fair features field crop competitions, 4-H exhibits and competitions, horse, pony and sheep shows. Apple cider pressing demonstrations, crafts, and a flea market are other highlights.
usually held the second weekend in September

Fall Fair

Midland

This agricultural fair features craft displays, horse pulls, and a junior fair section.

usually held Friday and Saturday, the second weekend in September

Fall Fair

Mildmay

The country spirit is alive at this fair. Events include horse, cattle, and poultry shows, agricultural exhibits and a midway.

usually held Friday and Saturday, the second weekend in September

Fall Fair

Mount Forest — (519) 323-1258

Country fair features here include horse and cattle shows, tug-of-war, Queen of the Fair Contest, and agricultural exhibits.

usually held the second weekend in September

Fall Fair

New Hamburg

Ben Hur would be proud of the folks who compete in chariot races at the New Hamburg Fall Fair. The fair also includes livestock competitions, heavy horse pulls, and horse shows.

usually held on Friday and Saturday, the second weekend in September

Antique Show and Sale

Niagara Falls

You're sure to find some unique Christmas gifts here.

usually held the second weekend in September

Six Nations Indian Fair

Brantford

Enjoy this agricultural fair which has a native people's atmosphere. Features are a midway, Indian crafts, Indian dancers, agricultural exhibits, western events, and school displays.

usually held the second weekend in September

Fall Fair

Orillia

Enjoy the excitement of a 6 horse driving competition, watch an antique threshing display, see the horse, cattle, and sheep shows, and stroll along the midway. All this and more is possible at the Orillia Fall Fair.

usually held the second weekend in September

Durham Central Exhibition

Orono

This large agricultural fair features a holstein show, a tractor pull, a poultry show, harness racing, wagoneering, and a midway.

usually held the second weekend in September

Fall Fair

Owen Sound

This Georgian Bay community celebrates the harvest with horse, cattle, pony and poultry shows, 4-H exhibits, and a midway.

usually held the second weekend in September, Thursday through Saturday

The Fall Fair of Central Lambton County

Petrolia — (519) 882-0488

See the agricultural heritage of this region at their fall fair. There are livestock exhibits, entertainment, a parade, and a midway.

usually held the second weekend in September

Fall Fair

Picton

This agricultural fair features horse, cattle, goat, and poultry shows, crafts, agricultural products, and a midway.

usually held the second weekend in September

Fall Fair

Port Hope

Many 'Hopers' will be hoping for the blue ribbon in horse, cattle, and fiddling competitions. Come cheer them on!

usually held the second weekend in September

Fall Fair

Powassan

This agricultural fair features cattle, horse, and poultry shows, baking and crafts, flower and vegetable shows, and a midway.

usually held the second weekend in September

Fall Fair

Renfrew

This agricultural fair features cattle shows, light and heavy horse shows, a steer and barrow sale, plus a midway, and grandstand entertainment.

usually held the second weekend in September

Green tomatoes

It always seems there are more tomatoes than can be used, whether they're from your backyard garden, or the farmer's market. As the frost approaches, don't worry about those unripened green tomatoes — there are plenty of possibilities for them.

Green tomatoes do not have to be turned to red to be eaten. Try frying them with onions — they're terrific with fried eggs for breakfast! There are also many green tomato pickle and relish recipies available: here's one you can try this fall.

Green Tomato Pickles

Cut 4 quarts green tomatoes, 6 large onions, and 6 sweet red peppers into thin slices. Mix in 1 cup pickling salt and leave overnight. The next day, drain the vegetables and rinse them well in several changes of cold water. Using a large pot, boil 5 cups of cider vinegar and 5 cups of white sugar with 1 teaspoon each of celery seed, cinnamon cloves, cayenne, mustard seeds, and allspice. Add the vegetables and boil the mixture for about 30 minutes. Be sure to stir it frequently to prevent sticking and to ensure even cooking. Pack the mixture into 6 hot, sterilized pint jars.

Agricultural Fair

Richmond

This large country fair has not sacrificed charm for size. Features include livestock shows and judging, a craft show, sports events, and a midway.
usually held the second weekend in September

Fall Fair

Shelburne — (519) 925-3115

'Fiddleville' has an agricultural side as well as a musical one, and Shelburne proves that with livestock shows, horse races, craft displays, and an antique car display.
usually held the second weekend in September, Friday and Saturday

Fall Fair

Spencerville

This fall fair features horse and cattle shows, 4-H shows, and a midway.
usually held the second weekend in September, Friday and Saturday

Fall Fair

Stisted (Twp. in Muskoka Cty.)

Enter in some of the races and contests at this harvest celebration.
usually held Friday and Saturday, the second weekend in September

Fall Fair

Sundridge

The wonderful colours of fall will be all around you as you head for this agricultural fair. Features include horse and cattle shows, crafts, and a variety night.
usually held the second weekend in September

Fall Fair

Tavistock — (519) 655-2315

There are horse shows, livestock competitions, crafts, and local talent.
usually held the second weekend in September, Friday and Saturday

Fall Fair

Uxbridge

Events at this agricultural fair include a tractor pull, horse shows, horse pulls, greyhound races, dairy cattle, beef cattle, sheep and goat shows, plus a steam era show.
usually held the second weekend in September

Fall Fair

Wiarton

This fall fair features horse shows, 4-H exhibits, a dairy show, crafts, and baking.
usually held Friday and Saturday, the second weekend in September

Caboto Club Grape Festival

Windsor — (519) 252-8383

Celebrate the grape with bands, dancing, cheese, and lots of wine.
usually held the second weekend in September

Fall Fair

Wyoming — (519) 845-3974

At this agricultural fair you'll find pet shows, cattle and swine judging, crafts and a midway.
usually held Friday and Saturday, the second weekend in September

Fall Fair

Sydenham

This agricultural exhibit is held at the Sydenham Central School and has been held annually for over 125 years.
usually held the second Friday in September

Lobster Fest

Brantford — (519) 753-4317

The Rotary Club sponsors this feast of lobster and roast beef. There's entertainment and dancing, too.
usually held the second Saturday in September

Flea Market

Burford — (519) 449-2446

No fleas, just lots of bargains.
usually held the second Saturday in September

Fall Fair

Iron Bridge

The Lions Hall and Community Centre is the site of this country fair which features vegetable and cattle shows, home baking, and crafts.
usually held the second Saturday in September

Fall Fair

Kirkton

This one-day fair will capture your city-heart away. Activities include livestock shows and competitions, flowers, home baking, and 4-H exhibits.
usually held the second Saturday in September

Tasty trash

Junk food addicts take note. Now you can get a garbage eating permit — for pigs. Sometimes hogs are fed selected garbage from restaurants, but only with a permit from the Canada Department of Agriculture Health of Animals Branch. And all the garbage food scraps must be cooked at 100°C for 30 minutes.

Fall Fair

Emsdale

This quaint country fair features horse shows, and an evening dance with a fiddle contest.

usually held the second Saturday in September

Art Festival

Grimsby — (416) 945-3246

There are 300-400 exhibitors at this show.

usually held the second Saturday in September

Binder Twine Festival

Kleinburg

This country fair was started by a shop-keeper who encouraged business by inviting farmers who bought their binder twine from him to a fall celebration. That's no longer a requirement for entry — just a love of the country.

Binder twine, by the way, is what holds bales of hay together.

usually held the second Saturday in September

Fall Fair

McKellar

Come to McKellar for a day of country good times. There's lots going on to keep you smiling — parade, horse and cattle show, fiddle and step-dance competitions, and a square dance.

usually held the second Saturday in September

Fall Fair

Middleville

Events at this one day fair include a flower show, homebaking, crafts display, light and heavy horse show, plus a home cooked turkey dinner, and dance in the evening.

usually held the second Saturday in September

Fall Fair

Neustadt

There are many interesting agricultural exhibits plus horse and cattle shows, flower shows, and a parade.

usually held the second Saturday in September

Grape Festival

Oakville — (416) 845-3483

Celebrate the wonderful grape! Ethnic dancers, family activities, musical entertainment, and, of course, wine!

usually held the second Saturday in September

Fall Fair

Oakwood

This one-day fair features the Victoria County Holstein Show, junior fair exhibits, and a dance in the evening.

usually held the second Saturday in September

Fall Fair

Severn Bridge

Two of the main events at this one day agricultural fair are the Queen of the Fair Contest, and the heavy horse drawing match. There are fireworks in the evening.

usually held the second Saturday in September

Halton Hilly Half-Hundred Bicycle Tour

Burlington — (416) 689-6126

This delightful tour of Lowville, Campbellville, Carlisle and Kilbride starts from Hwy 5 and the Guelph Line.

usually held the second Sunday in September

Annual Flower and Vegetable Show

Collingwood

All your favourites and more will be shown at the Trinity United Church.

usually held the second Saturday in September

Muskoka Cavalcade of Colour

Huntsville, Gravenhurst, and Bracebridge

Celebrate the turning of the leaves with these three towns. There are street dances, turkey dinners and fireworks as the leaves change from green to crimson.

mid-September through mid-October

Fall Fair

Beeton

Events at this fair include light and heavy horse shows, cattle, sheep and swine shows, grain and vegetable shows, and crafts.

usually held Tuesday and Wednesday, the third week in September

Antique Show and Sale

Belleville

St. Andrews Presbyterian Church, Victoria Ave., hosts this annual antique event.

usually held Wednesday and Thursday, the third week in September

Fall Fair

Brussels

At this country fair you'll find a midway, horse and pony races, horse shows, cattle, sheep and swine shows, crafts and agricultural exhibits.

Now, isn't all that worth a mid-week break?

usually held Tuesday and Wednesday, the third week in September

Fall Fair

Dungannon

Start your weekend early at this agricultural fair — after all, the fresh air will do you good! Features here include horse, cattle and goat shows, 4-H exhibits, a log sawing contest, crafts and baking, and a midway.

usually held Wednesday, Thursday and Friday, the third week in September

Cheese and Wine Festival

Ingersoll — (519) 485-4930

Get your feet wet (and maybe purple!) in the Mayor's Grape Stomp! There's also a parade, tasting parties, dances, and many grape times.

usually held the third week in September

Fall Fair

Paisley

There are horse, cattle, goat and sheep shows, plus agricultural exhibits, at this fair.

usually held Monday and Tuesday, the third week in September

Fall Fair

Rodney — (519) 785-2493

At the Rodney Fall Fair there are cattle and horse shows, tractor pulls, horse pulls, grandstand shows, and a midway.

usually held Tuesday and Wednesday, the third week in September

Fall Fair

Seaforth

This fall fair features horse and livestock shows, produce displays, crafts, baking, and a midway.

usually held Thursday and Friday, the third week in September

Fall Fair

Aberfoyle — (519) 836-2259

This agricultural fair has english and western horse shows, livestock shows, crafts, a horse pull, baking, and a midway.

usually held the third weekend in September, Friday and Saturday

Fall Fair

Ancaster — (416) 648-6198

This lively fair features the largest school fair in Ontario plus harness racing, horse and livestock shows, agricultural products competition, crafts, and a midway.

usually held the third weekend in September

Antique Show and Sale

Barrie

This annual event attracts dealers and buyers from across the province.

usually held the third weekend in September

Preserving wild plants and flowers

Many of the beautiful plants found in the woods can be preserved to last in your home. Most methods are easy, require little expense or equipment, and produce amazing results.

Pressed Flowers

You can press flowers between the pages of a weighted book, an old telephone book (not the yellow pages), or in a flower press, which can be purchased in craft and hobby stores. The flowers should be left undisturbed for at least a week; thin, non-fleshy flowers work best. Pressed flowers look lovely in an antique frame.

Oven-dried Flowers

You can dry wild plants in the oven, on low heat (140°C/250°F). The drying time varies depending on the plant; when they feel dry, they are done. Woodsy plant materials, rather than delicate flowers, are best suited to this method.

Detergent Method

This is a cheap method which keeps colours bright. Fill a container (an empty coffee can works well) with laundry detergent and bury a flower in it. When the plant is dry, you can you use the soap in your wash.

Fall Fair

Bolton

There are large competitions in cattle, poultry, swine, sheep, goats, and field crops at this fair. Other features include western horse shows, beer gardens and entertainment.
usually held the third weekend in September

Fall Fair

Carp

See those wonderful Clydesdale horses here. There are also light and heavy horse shows, beef and dairy cattle shows, sheep, swine and goat shows, an antique display, and a midway.
usually held Friday and Saturday, the third weekend in September

Fall Fair

Donnybrook (dispersed rural community in East and West Wawanosh Twp. in Huron Cty.)

There s lots to see and do here — horse shows, tug-of-war, craft shows, and a parade are just some of the choices.
usually held the third weekend in September

Fall Fair

Drumbo — (519) 463-5463

Drumbo has all the favourite country fair events — horse and cattle shows, a craft show and sale, a midway, a tug-of-war, and 4-H exhibits.
usually held the third weekend in September

Fall Fair

Durham

Celebrate harvest time at this old fashioned country fair. Events include horse and livestock shows, vegetable displays, a horseshoe pitching contest, 4-H exhibits, and a midway.
usually held Friday and Saturday, the third week in September

Fall Fair

Exeter — (519) 235-2438

At this agricultural fair you'll find 4-H projects on display, horse shows, and school exhibits. On the Sunday, there's a musical Jamboree.
usually held the third weekend in September

Fall Fair

Glencoe — (519) 287-5815

This fair has a variety show, livestock shows, and a midway.
usually held the third weekend in September

Split Rail Festival

Flesherton

Step into the past — this festival is based on old-time lifestyles and crafts. There are demonstrations of rope making, rug hooking, quilting, and spinning, plus an antique car display, a turkey shoot, and entertainment.
usually held the third weekend in September

Fall Fair

Forest — (519) 873-5228

This community celebrates harvest time with a truly old-time country fair. Events include horse and livestock shows, 4-H exhibits, horse races, and a midway.
usually held Friday and Saturday, the third weekend in September

Fall Fair

Grand Valley

At this fair you can start the day right with a pancake breakfast, then watch the horse and livestock shows, view some of the agricultural exhibits, and go for a ride on the midway.
usually held Friday and Saturday, third weekend in September

Fall Fair

Harriston — (519) 338-3344

This fair features horse, cattle, calf and sheep shows, 4-H exhibits, crafts and a midway. And there's lots of good baking that you can bring home.
usually held Friday and Saturday, the third weekend in September

Fall Fair

Huntsville

The colours of fall will surround you as you enjoy horse shows, poultry shows, a horseshoe pitching contest, and agricultural exhibits.
usually held the third weekend in September

Antique and Art Sale

Kingston

The Portsmouth Olympic Harbour Building is the site of this annual show and sale.
usually held Friday and Saturday, the third weekend in September

Fall Fair

Lindsay

This large agricultural fair boasts over 33,000 sq. ft. of exhibition area. In that space you'll find horse, cattle, sheep and swine shows, agricultural displays, farm machinery displays, and entertainment.
usually held the third weekend in September

Fall Fair

Madoc

At this large agricultural fair there are livestock, dairy and horse shows, crafts, agricultural exhibits, and entertainment.
usually held the third weekend in September

Fall Fair

Milton — (416) 335-9210

This fair features a midway, horse shows, horse races, arts and crafts, antique displays, and home baking.
usually held the third weekend in September

Fall Fair

Milverton — (519) 595-8381

Join in this traditional harvest celebration, located in the heart of Mennonite country. Here you'll find old-fashioned cooking, crafts, and custom designed quilts. Agricultural events include horse and livestock shows, and the 4-H club exhibits. There is also local talent and a midway.
usually held Friday and Saturday, the third weekend in September

Fall Fair

Oro (Twp. in Simcoe Cty.)

You can see exciting chariot and chuckwagon races here. There are also horse shows, cattle shows, sheep shows, horseshoe pitching contests, and agricultural exhibits.
usually held Friday and Saturday, the third weekend in September

Fall Fair

Parkhill

This community's fall celebration offers a variety of country events. There are agricultural exhibits, baking and craft displays, harness racing, a talent show, horse and cattle shows, and a Fair Queen Contest.
usually held the third weekend in September

Fall Fair

Rocklyn

This fair features a tractor driving contest, a bicycle rodeo, 4-H exhibits, and livestock shows.
usually held Friday and Saturday, the third weekend in September

Fall Fair

Stratford — (519) 271-5130

The Perth County Holstein and Swine Championship shows are featured here, along with horse shows, school exhibits, crafts, a kiddies' farm, and entertainment.

usually held the third weekend in September

Fall Fair

Thorndale — (519) 461-1046

At this fair you'll find chuckwagon races, dairy and beef cattle shows, a tug-of-war, 4-H exhibits, antique displays, horse shows, and entertainment.

usually held the third weekend in September

Fall Fair

Chatsworth

There are many different events packed into this one-day fair — a flea market, livestock shows, 4-H exhibits, baking demonstrations, crafts and antiques.

usually held the third Saturday in September

Octoberfest

Oakville — (416) 845-4551

German food and entertainment await you at the Oakville Arena.

usually held the third Saturday in September

Cider Day

Peterborough

Celebrate the apple harvest with cider, at Century Village.

usually held the third Sunday in September

Niagara Grape and Wine Festival

St. Catharines — (416) 688-0212

Join in this celebration of the ripening of the grapes. The wine flows through ten days of wine and cheese parties, ethnic concerts, athletic events, and parades. There are daily tours of the vineyards and wineries.

usually held the last week in September

Fall Fair

Langton — (519) 875-2458

What a perfect excuse for a mid-week break! There's a horse and pony show, nail driving contest, tobacco grading competition, and a pony pull.

usually held Wednesday, the last week in September

Annual Cavalcade of Colour Antique Show and Sale

Bala

Shop and browse in a colourful fall setting.

usually held the last weekend in September

The Alvinston Fair

Alvinston — (519) 898-5517

This fair features horse, cattle, and swine shows, craft and cooking exhibits, entertainment, and a midway.

usually held Friday and Saturday, the last weekend in September

Fall Fair
Bobcaygeon

There's a world of country events here — horse, cattle, sheep, and goat shows, agricultural exhibits, and log sawing and horseshoe pitching contests.
usually held the last Friday and Saturday in September

Fall Fair
Caledonia

The emphasis at this fair is on 4-H and Junior Farmer displays of grains, sheep, cattle, horses, fruits and vegetables, and over 7,000 exhibits.
usually held the last weekend in September

Annual Antique Show and Sale
Elora

There are many interesting and useful items here for sale or viewing.
usually held the last weekend in September

St. Paul's Arts and Crafts Exposition
Fort Erie — (416) 871-4158

St. Paul's Parish is host to this show and sale of a wide range of arts and crafts. There are also how-to demonstrations.
usually held the last weekend in September

Fall Fair
Georgetown — (416) 877-4207

This country fair features light and heavy horse shows, cattle shows, 4-H exhibits, crafts and a midway.
usually held the last weekend in September, Friday and Saturday

The straight and narrow

One of the most familiar things to anyone who drives along the highways in rural Ontario is the sight of a lone speck in the distance, ploughing the fields and the sound of a faintly droning tractor. The idea of a farmer doing the same thing before thousands of spectators is hard to imagine. Yet that's what happens at Ontario's International Ploughing Match.

The International Ploughing Match was established in 1913 on a farm that is now the site of Sunnybrook Hospital in Toronto. Now the Match is held on a farm or group of farms in a different county of Ontario each year.

The Match is one of Ontario's most popular agricultural events. As many as 100,000 people turn up to watch competitors of all ages vie for $35,000 in prize money. The event requires a site of over 100 acres and a huge tented city is erected for facilities and exhibits.

Ploughing matches were originally held as part of fall agricultural fairs in the mid-nineteenth century. One of the earliest recorded matches was held in Toronto in 1846 as part of the first provincial exhibition. And just to give you an idea of what the city was like then, the match was held on a farm in the Yonge and St. Clair area.

In the early days, ploughs were almost exclusively drawn by horse and oxen. But now, the International Ploughing Match is one of the few places where this kind of ploughing is practiced. It is rarely seen on working farms.

Although the Ploughing Match is independent of fall fairs, it includes many events similar to those held at fairs. In addition to ploughing competitions, it features a parade, cooking and craft competitions, a horse show, a flower show, a fashion show, and a horseshoe pitching tournament.

The festivities also include a beauty pageant with a difference. Contestants in the Queen of the Furrow Pageant are judged on their ploughing ability as well as their personality and appearance. Their furrows have to be straight and even, just like anyone else's.

The farming community in the county where the Match is being held also has an opportunity to get involved. The Ploughman's Association sponsors a Farmstead and Home Improvement Competition. People are encouraged to clean, repair, and paint their homes and farm buildings in preparation for the big event. All competitors are recognized at a banquet held in the weeks preceding the Match.

The Match is usually held in late September. Contact the Ontario Ministry of Agriculture and Food for further information.

Fall Fair

Ilderton

Most country fair activities featured here at this large agricultural celebration.

usually held the last weekend in September, Friday and Saturday

Pennsylvania — German Days

Kitchener — (519) 744-5382

The Doon Pioneer Village is the place to be for Pennsylvania-German food, crafts, and demonstrations of apple butter and cheese making

usually held the last weekend in September

Markham Fair

Markham

You're sure to get that old-time country feeling here. There are home made jams, jellies, and pickles, judging of horse and cattle shows, trotting races, farm machinery displays, crafts, local merchant's booths, and a midway.

usually held the last weekend in September

Fall Fair

Metcalfe

At this large agricultural fair you'll find horse and livestock shows, crafts, horse pulls, 4-H exhibits, and a midway.

usually held the last weekend in September

Annual Antique Show and Sale

Sarnia

This annual event has a wide range of relics from the area.

usually held the last weekend in September

Fall Fair

Ripley

Believe it or not, this is one of the best country fairs around! Features here are shows of grain, vegetables, fruit and flowers, baking, canning, crafts, horse and livestock shows, square dancing, and a parade.

usually held the last Friday and Saturday in September

Fall Fair

Roseneath

The very essence of country fairs comes to life here. Enjoy horse and livestock shows, horseshoe pitching contests, flower, fruit and vegetable displays, 4-H exhibits, crafts, and baking.

usually held the last Friday and Saturday in September

Fall Fair

Wainfleet — (416) 834-9765

This agricultural fair features horse and livestock shows, craft and quilting demonstrations, farm exhibits, a log sawing contest, and antiques.

usually held the last Friday and Saturday in September

Annual Fair

Wallacetown — (519) 762-5252

This town's harvest celebration includes 4-H exhibits, cattle, sheep, swine and horse shows, crafts, and a midway.

usually held the last Friday and Saturday in September

Fogolar Furlan Club Grape Festival

Windsor — (519) 966-2230

There's music, cheese and lots of wine. What more could you want?

usually held the last weekend in September

Fall Fair

Houghton (dispersed rural community in Haldimand-Norfolk Cty.)

Start your weekend early at this harvest celebration. You'll enjoy the nail driving contest, pet show, arts and crafts, baked goods, livestock shows and agricultural exhibits.

usually held the last Friday in September

Fall Fair

McDonald's Corners

There are horse shows and handcrafts at this one-day fair.

usually held the last Saturday in September

Annual Craft Festival

Paris

Many talented craftspeople show and sell their work here.

usually held at the end of September

Apple, Butter and Cheese Festival

Wellesley — (519) 656-2920

Start the day right with a pancake and sausage breakfast: you'll need the energy! There's a farmer's market, street mall and art show to be strolled through, tours of farms and an apple butter and cider mill to take in, and a horse shoe pitching competition to watch.

usually held the last Saturday in September

Bicycle Tour of Pioneer Country

Cambridge (Galt) — (519) 689-6126

This tour leaves Victoria Park in the morning. There is a registration fee.

usually held the fourth Sunday in September

Ciderfest

Egmondville — (519) 527-0160

Housed in the Van Egmond house (circa 1840) are sausage making and cider making demonstrations, crafts, and entertainment. And lots of hot apple cider will give you a warm glow.

usually held the last Sunday in September

Algoma Fall Festival

Sault Ste. Marie

This two-week festival features music, theatre, film and dance, plus an arts and crafts show and sale.

usually held late September through early October

Simcoe County Quilt and Rug Fair

Midhurst — (705) 728-3721

Because of the length of time it takes to complete a handmade quilt or rug, this fair is held every other year. Call the Simcoe County Museum to check the date.

usually held in October

Fall Fair

Caradoc — (519) 264-1275

At this fair you'll find horse shows, western games, crafts, a tug-of-war, a midway, and lots of good times.

usually held the first Friday and Saturday in October

Craft Show

Port Colborne — (416) 834-7424

This show and sale features local artists demonstrating their work.

usually held in October

Octoberfest

Welland — (416) 732-7515

A traditional German party with bands, food, beer, and dancing is held here.

usually held in Ocotber

Harvest Festival

Milton — (416) 878-4131

Apples are the focus of attention in this festival, held at the Mountsberg Wildlife Centre. There are cider making demonstrations, cider for sale, and apple games.

usually held Saturdays, Sundays, and holidays in October

Cider Days

Port Rowan — (519) 586-2201

Sip apple cider while watching a restored press squeeze every drop of juice out of an apple. There is also a display of modern cider making methods, plus cider for sale. Backus Conservation Area is where it all happens.

usually held early in October

Norfolk County Fair

Simcoe — (519) 426-7280

This harvest celebration features horse and cattle shows, sheep, goat, and poultry shows, fruit, vegetable and flower shows, 4-H exhibits, grandstand shows, and a midway.

usually held the first week of October

Fall Art Show

Niagara Falls — (416) 358-6959

This is an annual juried display of arts by local talent.

usually held the first two weeks in October

Annual Tobaccofest

Aylmer — (519) 773-3445

This community celebrates the tobacco harvest with festivities such as a trailer rally.

usually held the first weekend in October, Friday and Saturday

Fall Fair

Brigden — (519) 864-1718

There is a wide variety of events here — horse, cattle and goat shows, chariot races, agricultural exhibits, and a parade.

usually held the first weekend in October

Fall Fair

Burford

Features at this fair include chariot and chuck wagon races, agricultural exhibits, horse shows, poultry shows, goat shows, crafts and a midway.

usually held the first weekend in October

Pioneer Fall Festival

Napanee

Step back into the days of your forefathers in Napanee. Some of the attractions are bake sales, bazaars, an old fashioned market, craft demonstrations and sales, square dancing, and an antique farm machinery display. This all takes place at the Napanee Mall.

usually held throughout October

Fall Fair

Elmvale

Friendly country feelings abound here. You'll find livestock shows, agricultural exhibits, crafts, and great home cooked meals.

usually held the first Friday and Saturday in October

Fall Fair

Erin — (519) 927-5446

This large agricultural fair features tractor pulls, horse and cattle shows, farm exhibits, and a midway.

usually held the first weekend in October

Fall Fair

Gorrie — (519) 335-3269

This fall fair features horse shows, agricultural exhibits, and a midway.

usually held the first weekend in October

Fall Fair

Norwood

At this fair you'll find livestock and poultry shows, light and heavy horse shows, a pony pull, agricultural exhibits, and a midway.

usually held the first weekend in October

Winter Fair

Ottawa

This major agricultural fair features holstein shows, horse shows, 4-H exhibits, and farm displays.

usually held the first weekend in October

The time is ripe

Most people are able to distinguish between strawberries and raspberries at an early age. However, although they know which is which, they may not know which is when. Is it strawberries in July and raspberries in June or the other way around?

Many of Ontario's fruit and vegetables have short harvesting seasons and it's easy to confuse or forget when they're in season. Here's a guide to when various kinds of fruits and vegetables in Ontario can be harvested.

The list is useful, though not infallible. Dates given are approximate and will fluctuate due to weather, region of Ontario, and size of the crops. If yields are small, seasons may be shorter than what is indicated simply because the crops have been picked out. Some of the produce is susceptible to frost and an early frost will limit the season.

This guide will be especially useful to those who are interested in visiting one of Ontario's pick-your-own produce farms. These farms give you the opportunity to enjoy high quality, economical fruit and vegetables with the fun of picking them yourself. Many of these farms are listed in The Towns section of this book. However, a complete list of them is available from the Ontario Ministry of Agriculture and Food. It publishes a booklet each year that lists over 200 farms. It's located at 801 Bay St. in Toronto.

Vegetables

Asparagus — mid-May to mid-June

Beans (green and yellow) — mid-June through September

Beets —July through September

Broccoli — June and July as well as late August into November

Cabbage — June into November

Carrots — July to mid-October

Cauliflower — mid-June into November

Celery — mid-July into November

Corn (sweet) — late July to late September

Cucumbers — July through September

Lettuce — June to October, depending on variety

Onions (green) — mid-June to frost

Parsnips — September to mid-October

Peas — mid-May through June

Peppers — early August through September

Potatoes — July to early September

Radishes — early June through September

Spinach — early June to late September

Squash (summer) — July through September

Tomatoes — mid-July through September

Turnips — July to mid-October

Fruits

Apples — most varieties are available from August through October

Cherries — different kinds are available at different times from July to early August.

Gooseberries — last 3 weeks in July

Grapes — September is the month for most grapes, however some varieties are available through October

Melons — most melons are available during August and September

Peaches — different varieties are available at different times from late July to mid-September

Pears — mid-August to mid-October

Plums — from late July through September

Raspberries — last 2 weeks of July

Strawberries — early June to early July

Fall Fair

Rockton — (519) 628-2165

This large agricultural fair features horse and livestock shows, 4-H displays, crafts, and a midway.
usually held the first weekend in October

Fall Fair

Teeswater

Join in this community's harvest celebration. Events include sheep, goat and poultry shows, heavy and light horse shows, horse and saddle races, and a midway.
usually held the first Friday and Saturday in October

Annual Antique Show and Sale

Jordan

You're bound to find something special at this show and sale, held at the Beacon Motor Hotel.
usually held the first Wednesday and Thursday in October

Octoberfest

Grimsby — (416) 945-3519

Enjoy oom-pah bands, German food, dancing, and beer, from noon till midnight.
usually held the first Saturday in October

Fall Fair

Highgate — (519) 678-3867

This one-day fair doesn't skimp on activities. There are horse and livestock shows, grain, vegetable, flowers, baking, craft displays, and 4-H exhibits.
usually held the first Saturday in October

Fall Fair

Tweed

At this fair you'll find a midway, horse and cattle shows, grains, seeds, vegetables, fruit, flower, and cheese displays, crafts, and baking.
usually held the first Friday and Saturday in October

Octoberfest

Windsor — (519) 969-3815

You're sure to enjoy this traditional German festival.
usually held the first and second weekend in October

Fall Fair

Woodbridge

There are lots of good country times to be had here — enjoy harness races, dog races, 4-H exhibits, grain, root and vegetable displays, crafts, and horse and livestock shows.
usually held the first weekend in October

Fall Fair

Tiverton

This agricultural fair has horse and livestock shows, field crop competitions, arts and crafts, baking and canning, and farm exhibits.
usually held the first Saturday in October

Come Close to Nature Hike

Varna — (519) 235-2610

See some autumn flora and fauna on this guided hike through the Bannockburn Wildlife Centre.
usually held the first Sunday in October

Bicycle Tour of Rice Lake

Cobourg

This tour takes you through some very pretty countryside.
usually held the first Sunday in October

Thanksgiving Festival and Craft Show

Jordan — (416) 892-2609

Celebrate this holiday with a service in a historic church and tours of historic buildings; watch an 1890 gristmill in action, and browse through the craft show and sale at Ball's Falls Conservation Area.
usually held Thanskgiving weekend

Thanksgiving Festival

Oakville — (416) 827-6911

Have a good, old-fashioned time at this Thanksgiving celebration. Bronte Creek Provincial Park is the place for pumpkin carving, apple bobbing, a steam engine display, apple cider making demonstrations, and corn husk dolls.
usually held Thanksgiving weekend

Octoberfest

Kitchener — Waterloo — (519) 576-0571

Ein prosit! Ein prosit! Raise your glass of draught and enjoy German food, dancing, and music. There are also bicycle races (no brew for this, please), flower shows, and a beauty pageant, as the whole town gets involved in this renowned event.
usually held the second week of October

Fall Fair

Walkerton

The frost is on the pumpkin and its time for a country fair! This one features horse and cattle shows, grain and vegetable displays, crafts, and entertainment.
usually held the second weekend in October

Octoberfest

Exeter

This community gets into the festive spirit with beer, German food, music, and dancing, at the South Huron Recreation Centre.
usually held the second Saturday in October

Pioneer Day

Jordan — (416) 562-5242

Festivities include pioneer crafts, cider making, a steam show, and pioneer games. When hunger strikes, there's a soup kettle and a Pennsylvania-German food tent.
usually held the second Saturday in October

Fall Colour Bicycle Tour

Kingston

Enjoy the colours of fall as you pedal along on this 80 km tour.
usually held the second Saturday in October

Migration Festival

Kingsville — (519) 733-2315

Look, up in the sky! Not for Superman, but for that famous 'V' formation. This three day festival salutes the Canada Goose with a parade, and entertainment. The Jack Miner Bird Sanctuary will provide the vantage points.
usually held in mid-October, depending on the geese

Annual Arts and Crafts in the Country

Belle River

Browse through this show and sale in a country setting.
usually held the third weekend in October

Christmas Country Fair

Saltford — (519) 524-2713

Get that holiday feeling, and get your Christmas shopping started, at this annual show and sale of local arts and crafts, and baking, held at the Saltford Valley Hall.

usually held the third weekend in October

Octoberfest

Brantford — (519) 753-5770

These German festivities are brought to you by the Lion's Club.

usually held the third Saturday in October

Harvest Festival

Niagara Falls — (416) 356-2521

Get your costumes out, it's that ghost and goblin time again! Craft shows, square dances, a marathon race, and harvest produce displays keep those beasties tame.

usually held the last week in October

Ciderfest

Port Stanley — (519) 782-3264

This country festival coincides with the local apple harvest.

usually held the last Friday in October

Arts and Crafts Exhibition

Acton — (519) 853-0805

This show and sale, located in the St. Alban's Parish Hall, features weaving, wood burning, and batik.

usually held the last Saturday in October

The Falling Leaves Frolic Bicycle Tour

Campbellville — (519) 689-6126

Catch all the fall colours as you pedal through this rolling countryside. What could be more peaceful? The tour starts from the Community Park.

usually held the last Sunday in October

Arts and Crafts Show and Sale

Orangeville

Over 40 professional and amateur craftspeople display their work in St. Marks Anglican Church.

usually held the last Saturday in October

Antique Show

Niagara-on-the-Lake

You're sure to find some unique items here.

usually held the first weekend in November

Arts and Crafts Show

Caledon East

The North Peel Lions Community Hall is the location of this annual event.

usually held the first Saturday in November

Royal Winter Fair

Toronto

The Royal Winter Fair, established in 1922, is billed as the largest indoor agricultural fair in the world.

It serves as a showcase for some of the finest agricultural products from Canada, the United States, and even some European countries. The fair also includes many educational displays, as well as a top-notch horse show, flower show, and food show.

usually held in mid-November

Craft Exhibition and Sale

Guelph

60 artisans from across Ontario are featured at the University of Guelph.

usually held the last Friday and Saturday in November

Christmas Show and Sale

Georgetown — (416) 877-0498

Find something for everyone on your Christmas shopping list. Choose from crafts such as pottery, weaving, and pewter.

usually held the last Saturday in November

Travel notes

The Towns

Aberfoyle

There's a fine meal awaiting you in Aberfoyle. The **Aberfoyle Mill** specializes in homemade food and is furnished with the rustic flavour of pine beams and a large stone fireplace. And should you happen to dine there on a weekend, it would be worth your while to visit the **Aberfoyle Antique Market** which is open on Sundays from May to October. Just south of Aberfoyle in Freelton, there's an antique store with an intriguing name. **Mystique Antiques** is located south of Highway 401, off Highway 6 N.

Acton

It seems that Acton and surrounding areas are good places to pick up some country crafts and cooking. **Elm Tree Farm** in Acton offers wool for hand weaving, hasty notes, and home baking to it's customers. If you're travelling south of Acton, **Eden Place Handcrafts** in Eden Mills might have some things to interest you also. It features weaving, pottery, jewellery, and leatherwork and is open afternoons, including Sunday.

If you're headed north of Acton, don't feel left out. Just past Ballinsfad on Halton Rd. 3 (exit 40 on Highway 401) you'll find **Graham's Apple Farm**. Between mid-June and mid-October it features pick-your-own strawberries or apples. They also have a market from September through March that sells fresh apple cider.

Algonquin Park

If you need a bit of a break from all the vigorous activities in Algonquin Park, why not slow the pace down a little with an educational visit to one of the park's exhibits. The **Algonquin Pioneer Logging Exhibit** is located just inside the east gate on Highway 60. You can follow the history of logging in the park through displays, models, and an audio-visual presentation. It's open daily from mid-June to mid-October, and from May 1 to mid-June on weekends only.

The **Algonquin Park Museum** features displays of fish, wildlife, and geology. It's located in the southern part of the park and is accessible by Highway 16. Information about the park's history and resource management is presented in an audio-visual program. This museum is open during the same times of year as the logging exhibit.

Alliston

Although Alliston may be known for its potatoes and its potato festival, it is also known as a good place to pick up some pottery. **Alliston Pottery** is a factory outlet and showroom located at 83 Dufferin St.

Before you get too far away from Alliston you should check out some of the fine dining spots nearby. **The Globe Restaurant** in Rosemont is housed in a wooden building built in the 1800s. You'll also find a country inn in Loretto. The **Gypsy Lane Inn** serves both tea and dinners in a setting where you can enjoy a beautiful view of the Hockley Valley. It's a good idea to have reservations.

Alton

One of the highlights of a trip through Alton is **Mackenzie's Mill.** This fully restored knitting mill was built in 1881 and has walls two feet thick. The mill site has antique shops, boutiques, an art gallery, a bakery shop, an auction hall, and a restaurant. **The Millpond Inn** serves lunch, English tea, and dinner.

Alton is also the home of **The Millcroft Inn,** an elegant, gourmet country dining spot. It's another restored mill, with the dining room overlooking the mill-pond. The 100-acre wooded lot surrounding the Inn lends itself beautifully to quiet after-dinner strolls, or cross-country skiing.

Ancaster

One of the highlights of a trip to Ancaster is a visit to the **Ancaster Old Mill.** You can tour the mill and watch wheat being ground in the nineteenth century manner. And to prove to yourself that the old method is still efficient, you can buy the resulting loaves of bread at the bakery in the miller's house. You can also enjoy a fine country meal in the nearby **Old Mill Inn.** The dining room provides a rustic atmosphere and a great view of the mill itself, the miller's house, two waterdrops, and the mill pond.

On your way out of town, you may want to take advantage of some nearby farm produce outlets. **Bennett's Apple and Cider,** 944 Highway 53 E., specializes in apples and fresh cider, as well as potatoes, summer fruits, and sweet corn. **Lindley's Fruit and Vegetables,** 219 Book Rd. W., specializes in pick-your-own strawberries, tomatoes, beans, peppers, and eggplant. You can reach it by taking Fiddler's Green Rd. south from Highway 53 to Book Rd.

Arkona

Arkona is the site of the beautiful Rock Glen Waterfalls. These waterfalls have provided some exciting scientific and historical finds as well as natural beauty. Early Indian pottery, semi-precious stones, and petrified wood fossils as old as 280 million years have been found in the area. These items and many others are now displayed in the **Arkona Lions Artifact Museum.** It's open year round in the afternoons except Mondays and Fridays.

After a day of soaking up some history in Arkona, you can enjoy some light summer theatre in Grand Bend, just north of Arkona. You'll find it at the **Huron County Playhouse** which is located in a renovated barn. Comedies and musicals are standard summer fare. The playhouse is located off the Blue Water Highway and operates during July and August.

If you're in the area on a Sunday during the summer, why not visit the **Pinery Flea Market?** It's located 3 km south of Grand Bend, on Highway 21.

Aylmer

Aylmer is known for its proximity to bird migration and nesting areas. You can watch the swans in the last two weeks of March, and the migration of waterfowl at the end of October and beginning of November, at the **Aylmer Wildlife Management Area.** Another exciting sight to see is the migration of the hawk in September, at the **Hawk Cliff Wildlife Agreement Area.**

If you're in Aylmer on a Sunday, you should check out the **Antique Fun Fair.** It's held on the second and fourth Sunday of every month at 505 Talbot E.

Bancroft

Why not take the children along when you go to the Bancroft Gemboree this August? You'll find several exciting things for them to enjoy in the area. **Pauze's Wildlife Centre,** 13 km north of town, includes over 150 exotic birds and animals to hold the children's attention. It's open seven days a week during July and August.

For those who would rather do something than watch, there are 3 and 20 km whitewater **River Raft Trips** from the Madawaka Kanu Camp. The camp is located 12 km north of Purdy off Highway 62. Trips are offered from Monday to Thursday during July and August, but it is wise to call ahead to confirm an adequate water flow.

Barrie

There's a wide variety of things to see and places to go in Barrie. Just 10 km northwest of town you'll find **Springwater Provincial Park.** The park is rich in wildlife and you'll see beavers, racoons, deer, and swans in their natural surroundings.

Shopping and browsing opportunities await you in town. There's a large antique shop called **Visible Past Antiques** and a craft gallery called **Artifact.** The craft store is located at 3 Berczy St. in the home of the proprietor. It features pottery, glass, wood, and fabrics. Just south of Barrie, via Highway 11, is Stroud, where you'll find another antique shop called **The Old Iron Kettle.** It's open on weekend afternoons.

Maude Koury's Steak House is one of Barrie's fine dining spots. This charming old restaurant is located in a cozy, old home. An outdoor patio makes it a very pleasant place to dine in summer.

Also in the summer, you can enjoy first-rate plays by **Gryphon Theatre.** Plays run in the modern, air-conditioned Georgian Theatre at 401 Duckworth St. The season runs from early July until early September.

Barry's Bay

One of the attractions of Barry's Bay in the winter is **Mount Madawaska,** a ski resort with both downhill and cross-country facilities.

Just 18 km south of Barry's Bay on Highway 62 at Combermere, is the **Madonna House Pioneer Museum.** The museum includes a fine collection of items from pioneer days such as farm implements and machinery. There is also an antique shop in the museum that's open daily except Wednesdays, year-round.

Belfountain

Belfountain has a variety of interesting shops. The **Belfountain Village General Store** carries Canadian and imported cheeses, natural foods, fresh coffee beans (including the store's own special blend), and various specialty foods. **Greens 'n Things** combines the best of two worlds with hand crafts and plants. **The Pine and Patchworks** also provides a two-sided approach with crafts and food. It features handmade quilts, early pine furniture, pottery, homemade preserves, and antipasto. Where crafts are concerned, custom work is their specialty. You can also snoop around for antiques in Belfountain. **Mary's Belfountain Store** features antiques and country furnishings, and **Log House Antiques,** 3 km south of town, carries country furniture and accessories.

Blind River

The paper this book is printed on depends on towns like Blind River. And to get the history of the lumber industry straight, why not visit the **Timber Village Museum?** This museum contains models and artifacts relating to the lumber industry. Other exhibits concern the rocks, minerals, and agriculture of the area. It's open from July 1 to Labour Day.

Bloomfield

There are some fine craft shops in Bloomfield. **The Old Schoolhouse Pottery** is one place where you can pick up some functional craft items. Another such place is the **Homecraft Museum,** which carries antique furniture. Although **The Workshop** has the most functional name, it carries some fun things for children; its specialties are wooden gifts and toys.

Blyth

If you're looking for some fun evenings in the summer, you'll find them at the **Blyth Summer Festival.** It features light, entertaining plays in an air-conditioned, renovated theatre. The theatre is located in the Blyth Memorial Hall on Highway 4; plays run daily except Sundays during July and August.

Look for good buys at **The Old Mill** factory outlet for leathers and woolens on Highway 4, 2 km south of town. Its stock includes leather, suede, and fur coats, sheepskin rugs, and wool blankets. It's open 7 days a week.

Bobcaygeon

Bobcaygeon is located on three islands surrounded by shallow rapids; "Bobcaygeon" means shallow rapids in the local Indian dialect. One of the best preserved log houses in North America can be found here. The house is known as **The Beehive** and was built in 1838. Tours can be arranged through the Beehive Country Club.

Another feature of Bobcaygeon is its many antique shops. **Raebinloft Antiques,** located at 22 King St. E., specializes in china, glassware, sterling silver, and discontinued flatware patterns. It's open from mid-June until Labour Day. Another store is **Bottle Shop Antiques** which is located at 100 Head St.

There are some other interesting shops located in Fenelon Falls, west of Bobcaygeon. **Livery Stable Antiques and Handicrafts** is located at 4 May St. and **Wicker Works** is nearby at 7 May.

If you're interested in Indian crafts there's a store near Buckhorn, to the east of Bobcaygeon. The **Whetung Craft Centre** is located 9 km off Highway 507, on Curve Lake Road. It's open daily, year round.

Bowmanville

You'll discover some real treats for children in Bowmanville. At the **Bowmanville Zoo,** youngsters are encouraged to mingle with a variety of exotic but tame animals. They'll find deer, llamas, peacocks, camels, elk, and zebras roaming through wide open spaces. Picnic facilities are available at the zoo as well as a playground and a pool. There's even something for the younger set at the **Bowmanville Museum.** Exhibits there include a doll and toy collection. It's open afternoons except Mondays, from late May to mid-October.

Bowmanville also has various things to offer adults. If you're into antique hunting you can try **R.A. O'Neil Antiques Ltd.,** at 16 King St. E. And on your way out of town it's certainly worth a visit to **Ted Watson Farms** where you can pick your own strawberries, raspberries, or apples in season. They're open from late June to late October. They're found on Highway 2, just west of town. Further west on Highway 2 is another farm where you can harvest your own produce in season. **Fred Eyman's Farm** in Courtice is open seven days a week from September until the frost. East of Bowmanville on Highway 35 is a must stop for antiques, crafts, and collectibles. The **Talisman Emporium** near Newcastle, is open Saturdays, Sundays, and holidays, and boasts over 30 dealers' booths.

Bracebridge

While you're in the Bracebridge area, why not visit **Gull Island,** in the southeast part of Lake Muskoka? The island is a bird sanctuary, inhabited by gulls of all kinds, as well as the famous blue heron.

In Baysville, there is a wide variety of craft items at a store called **The Croft.** Choose from ceramics, toys, handwoven clothes, wood, and jewellery. It's open daily except Saturdays from June to Labour Day, and on Saturdays only from Labour Day until Thanksgiving.

If you enjoy shopping for old furniture and antiques, you should visit **Second Hand Stuff,** west of Bracebridge on Highway 118. The large barn is open from May until October.

Brampton

Antique hunters will enjoy visiting Brampton. There's a weekly **Antique Auction** Monday nights at the Junior Farmer's Hall on Elliot St. (The auctions are not held during July and early August.) There are also some interesting antique dealers in Brampton including **M and M Antiques** at 220 Main St. N., and **Angus Gillespie Antiques** at 10 Core Crescent.

If you're feeling energetic, head for **The Country Apple Store** and pick some strawberries or apples. This farm also has a market where you can get already-picked fruit as well as fresh cider, honey, and frozen foods. To get there, take Mississauga Road north from Highway 401, go west on Steeles to the 5th line and turn north. There's another country market not far from Brampton at Norval. **Pine Valley Farms Garden Market** sells apples, homemade pies, pumpkins, and greenhouse plants. They're located on Highway 7, 8 km west of Brampton. There's yet another farm outlet in the Brampton area. **Appletree Farms Country Market** is about 20 km north of Brampton on Highway 10. It features pick-your-own strawberries and apples. It also has a market that is open daily, year round, and features fresh fruits and vegetables, and home baked pies.

Just past Norval on Highway 7 is Georgetown, where you'll find a good craft store. **Gallery House Sol,** at 45 Charles St., sells a variety of crafts including blown glass, ceramics, weaving, and batik.

There's also a country dining spot in Georgetown. **Hunter's Inn Country Restaurant** is situated in a century old house at 99 Mountainview Rd. The restaurant features an international lunch and dinner menu. It offers a special brunch on Sundays, but it's closed Tuesdays.

Brantford

Brantford is rich in history. It is named for Joseph Brant, the famed Six Nations Indian chief who led his people to this area. Indian culture is well represented at the **Woodland Indian Museum,** at 184 Mohawk St. The museum is part of the Woodland Indian Cultural Educational Centre, which includes a library and an audio-visual department. The museum houses many authentic Indian artifacts including clothing, hunting and fishing implements, musical instruments, and arts and crafts.

Brantford was also the home of Alexander Graham Bell, the inventor of the telephone. Visitors can tour the **Bell Homestead** which is furnished with many pieces from the nineteenth century. The house was the site of the first long distance call, from Brantford to Paris, Ontario, 100 km away. **The Brant County Museum** at 57 Charlotte St. includes displays of early telephone equipment used by Bell. It also includes pioneer articles such as old firearms, fire fighting equipment, farming tools, and pottery.

One of the more curious landmarks of Brantford is **The Octagon House.** There are many theories as to why this three-story house was built with eight sides. Some say it keeps witches away! In any case, this beautifully restored building now houses a country restaurant. Another interesting place to dine in Brantford is **The Iron Horse,** at 60 Market St. S. This building is a former railroad station that was built in 1896, and now houses railroad memorabilia. You can enjoy your meal in an old fashioned train coach, or an enclosed railway platform.

For a glimpse of the past you can take home with you, visit **Brantwood Antiques.** It's located at 992 Colborne St., and is open every day.

A stop worth making

One of the joys of travelling through rural Ontario in the summer is taking advantage of the fresh produce available at roadside stands.

Buying from roadside stands benefits you and the farmer. Chances are the produce will be fresher and more economical than what you are accustomed to. And since the farmer has assumed the functions of wholesaler, shipper, packer, and retailer, his costs are reduced and his profits increased. Everybody wins!

The atmosphere at a roadside stand is a pleasant change from that of the supermarket. The clinking of coins in a farmer's pocket is a much nicer sound than the whirrs and beeps of an electronic cash register.

Buying directly from a farmer is usually a more flexible transaction than buying from a large supermarket. In some cases, it seems that nothing short of a heart-rending story of how you are buying groceries for your eighty year old grandmother who lives alone and eats like a bird will convince a grocery store clerk to break a package into smaller units. That is, if you can find a clerk. At roadside stands this is rarely necessary. Produce is often not packaged at all, but if it is grouped in bunches or baskets, you need only specify the amount you want to the attendant.

The people who work at roadside stands are often members of the farmer's family and have a good knowledge of the produce they sell. They will often be able to provide you with tips on when certain items will be in season, different varieties of a particular fruit or vegetable, or even how to prepare the food you buy.

Prices are another area where roadside stands tend to be flexible. If you spot an item that is less than fresh or slightly bruised, you can often "haggle" for a reduced price. With small operations like roadside stands, rules and regulations like fixed prices are often replaced by common sense.

Brighton

There's a mixed bag of things to see and do in the Brighton area. It is close to **Presqu'ile Provincial Park,** which is an excellent place for observing bird migration in the spring and fall. During the summer, park authorities conduct free tours of the park, including early morning canoe trips through the marsh. The **Presqu'ile Provincial Park Museum** features displays concerning pioneer life as well as the natural history and wildlife of the region. It is located in a former lighthouse keeper's home on RR5 at Brighton. The museum is open daily from Victoria Day to Labour Day.

If you're travelling west of Brighton, the **Pine Springs Farm Roadside Market** on Highway 2 is an ideal spot to purchase apples, apple butter, fresh cider, vegetables, and honey. It's open from late July to December. If you continue on Highway 2 to RR4 you'll find **Dutch Oven Antiques.** Specialties there include art glass, early furniture, and fine china.

Should you be heading north on a Saturday, a visit to the **Old Warkworth Cheese Factory** would be a real treat. Cheese is one of Ontario's best-known products, and this place offers demonstrations of old-fashioned cheese-making methods every Saturday, from Victoria Day to Thanksgiving.

Brockville

In the Brockville area you can either pick your own food or have it served to you. **Clow's County Market,** on Highway 29, 5km north of town, lets you harvest your own strawberries, sweet corn, and tomatoes, when they're in season. They also sell vine crops, potatoes, and fresh fruit over the counter.

They're open daily from mid-May to the end of October.

For those who aren't quite so adventurous and yet still enjoy good food, stay in town and have a meal at the **Towne Haus Tavern,** at 32 Apple St. The restaurant is located in a home that was built in 1826. For a compromise between harvesting your own food and eating indoors, you can take advantage of the outdoor patio at the Towne Haus in the summer.

There are several craft stores in Brockville that you can visit. **Coach House** is located on Water St., **This and That Boutique** is found at 102 King St. W., and **Whitehorse Gift Shoppe** is located at 180 King St. W.

Burk's Falls

There are some fine craftspeople working in and around Burk's Falls. One of the major outlets for these people is **The Peanut Gallery** at 157 Ontario St. It features a wide variety of crafts ranging from ceramics to woodwork to metalwork. About 4 km north of Burk's Falls on Highway 11 and 4 km east at the sign is **Manivaldi Woodworking.** Here, they practise a unique Estonian woodworking craft that involves a method similar to that used in barrel-making; the finished products include buckets, planters, and furniture.

Burlington

Burlington's main attraction is the **Joseph Brant Museum.** The museum is an authentic reconstruction of the home of the former Six Nations Indian chief. It includes a gallery which focuses on the life of Brant, an Indian exhibit which features ritual masks, and an exhibit which contains items relating to the history of Burlington. The museum also houses temporary exhibits which often relate to art or the museum's

fine costume collection.

There's a veritable trove of Canadian crafts at **The Treasury** in Burlington. It features Indian and Inuit art as well as pottery and jewellery. The store is located at 2100 Lakeshore Rd.

Calabogie

Winter sports enthusiasts will appreciate the ski facilities at **Calabogie Peaks.** The hills are primarily intermediate terrain and both downhill and cross-country runs are found there. And after an invigorating day on the slopes, you can relax in front of the huge fireplaces of the **Whippletree Shanty.** This rustic village inn is a cozy place to dine in winter. An open air beer garden with a charcoal pit is a summer attraction of the Shanty.

While you can enjoy the effects of gravity at the ski slopes, you can defy it at **Magnetic Hill** in nearby Dacre. You'll be surprised to see your car roll uphill! Dacre is northwest of Calabogie and to get to the hill, go 2 km south of the junction of Highway 132 and 41 and look for signs.

Caledon

If you're at all interested in crafts, antiques, or old fashioned country foods, you'll love Caledon. The only problem will be where to begin. **Things Old and New and Town Crier Books** carries glassware and china, small pieces of furniture, and old books and printed matter. You can also ask for details about their monthly auction sales. They're located on Highway 10, just north of the stoplights in Caledon Village. **The Woodcraft Shop** located on RR2, offers handcrafted pine furniture and accessories, and arts and crafts. Another good place to look for

furniture is **Caledon Stables Antiques.** It specializes in both European and Canadian furniture and is found at George St. and Highway 10. It's open on Saturday and Sunday afternoons. Also open on Saturday and Sunday, as well as holidays, is the **Caledon Studio,** which sells semi-precious stones, cut, set, and polished.

Endesleigh Studios would be a good place to start switching from craft shopping to shopping for fine foods. It carries both. On the craft side of things, it specializes in pottery and dried floral arrangements. Food-wise, it stocks gourmet jams and jellies, herbs, and herb vinegars. It's found on Highway 10, south of the Forks of Credit Road. Another must stop for those who appreciate fine foods is **Granny's Country Store.** It's specialty is frozen gourmet foods.

Caledon East

Come and see the **Albion Hills Farm School of Spinning and Dyeing.** The school has a vegetable dyehouse modelled on those found in the Appalachian region of the United States. It is located on a farm where a flock of 200 Southdown sheep provide the wool for the operations. Why not follow your visit up with a meal at the **Caledon Inn,** two stone houses on the site of a 150 year old coach house? You might also want to visit two of the town's fine craft shops, **Daphne of Canada** and **Pinelea Farms.**

Caledonia

One of the best puns heard in years is the name of a fine Indian craft store — **Iroqrafts.** It features fur boots, leather vests, headbands, moccasins, birchbark and quill crafts, corn dolls, and parkas.

Another attraction in the Caledonia area is **Big Creek Boat Farm.** Located on RR2, the complex includes riverboat cruises, pony rides, farm animals, and picnic and playground facilities.

Earth tones

Wool is not the only fibre that can be spun into yarn. Silk from milkweed pods, some dog's hair, and flax, as well as worm silk and cotton, all produce yarn. And these natural fibres can be beautifully dyed with colours from various plants, flowers, and berries.

A visit to a natural dye house like the one in Caledon East can be an enjoyable and educational experience. Should it inspire you, your public library is a good place to find more information. Here are some sources and colours to get you thinking about this age-old craft.

Walnut hulls produce a light to dark brown colour; dandelion leaves and flowers produce a yellow to lime green dye; Queen Anne's Lace, that delicate, common wild flower, produces a golden yellow dye; pink comes from beet juice; blueberries make blue; onion skins produce a golden brown dye; and spinach leaves yield lime green.

Cambridge

Cambridge is a great place to shop for crafts and antiques. A most unusual store is the **Frog and Box Toy Co.** This rather unlikely sounding business carries a fascinating collection of handmade, large toys; the human figure toys are lifesize, some as tall as five foot seven inches! Another craft shop in Cambridge is **The Benchmark,** located at 640 Hespeler Road. Antique hunters will have a field day in this town — there's **Backyard Unlimited** at 13 Queen St. W., **Beckner's Antiques** at 7 Queen St. W., **Cambridge Antique and Collectors Centre** at 41 Water St. S., **Donaldson Antiques** at 13 Salisbury Ave., **Homestead Antiques** at 28 Colborne St., and **Patricia Korte Antiques** at 28 Queen St. W.

Clappison's Corners

If you enjoy browsing through old stuff, be sure to visit the **Circle M Ranch Flea Market.** It's located on Highway 5, 4 km west of Highway 6, and is open every Sunday.

Another place to visit in the area is **Belvedere Orchards.** They're open from August for pick-your-own apples. To get there, take Highway 6, 3 km north of town, turn east on the fifth concession and go in 1 km. They're open every day but Sundays.

Cobalt

Cobalt is an excellent place to learn more about the mining industry in Ontario. The Cobalt **Mining Museum** features early mining photographs and old mining tools. One of the most interesting pieces of equipment is the old fashioned mining helmets, with candles attached to them to provide light. The museum also includes a collection of large silver pieces found in the region. Geology buffs may also be interested in the large collection of fluorescent rocks. The museum can also supply you with information about **Mine Tours** offered by local firms.

Cobourg

There's a fine restaurant with an interesting story to it in Cobourg. It's **Marie Dressler's Birthplace,** the former home of one of Hollywood's funniest comediennes who co-starred with Wallace Beery in a number of films. The restaurant has several small dining rooms, one decorated in the Victorian style, with others decorated in an early Canadian style. During the summer, you can have your meal on the outdoor terrace.

Cochrane

Wood and steel are the keys to Cochrane. You can explore the forests and learn about the lumber industry as well as enjoy a great train ride and visit a railway museum. The **Polar Bear Express** is a day-long rail trip through rugged wilderness country accessible only by rail or air. Its destination is Moosonee, known as the gateway to the Arctic, on the west coast of James Bay. Upon arrival at Moosonee, you can take a boat to Moose Factory Island, Ontario's oldest permanent settlement which dates back 300 years; today, it's a good place to buy crafts. The Express runs from Monday to Thursday each week during July and August.

At the **Railway and Pioneer Museum** in Cochrane you can see old railway cars, photographs, and railway artifacts. The museum is open afternoons from June to Labour Day.

If you're interested in the lumber industry, there's the **Cochrane Enterprises Tour** which shows you how plywood is made, from logs to the finished product. The plant is located on Railway St. and is open on Mondays, Wednesdays, and Fridays from July 1 to Labour Day.

You'll see a different kind of woodworker if you walk along the **Muskeg Trail.** There's a beaver house and dam alongside the trail which is located 15 km west of Cochrane on the south side of Highway 11. It's open from spring thaw to fall freeze-up.

Collingwood

Many people think of Collingwood as a great place to go in the winter because of its ski area; but one shouldn't forget that it's also an exciting place in summer. The skiing facilities are put to good use with **The Great Slide Ride.** You ride the chairlift up Blue Mountain where you get a splendid view of Georgian Bay, then you whiz down a 900 metre track through the trees on a plastic sled. The sleds have brakes on them so you can slow down to enjoy the view or speed up and take banked curves at speeds up to 40 km per hour.

A slower paced but still interesting activity in Collingwood is a trip through the **Scenic Caves.** The caves are found at the top of the escarpment, which offers breathtaking views of the land to the north and east.

A big attraction for children in the Collingwood area is the **Candy Factory** on Highway 26, just west of town. Most of the candy sold there is made on the premises and you can watch it being made through observation windows. There's also a display of candy-making equipment from the past. In summer, the store has an outdoor patio where you can cool off with ice cream, pop, and frozen yogurt. Inside the store you can choose from chocolates, boiled candy, fudge, and nuts.

Flour power

Long before Ontarians harnessed the energy of Niagara Falls, they were taking advantage of water power. The most prominent reminders of this are the gristmills that still stand today in some Ontario towns.

Historians estimate that gristmills, used for grinding grain, were first built in the late 1700s. Dams were built on areas of fast flowing water such as river gorges. The water from the dams was directed down wooden troughs or chutes to wooden wheels. The force of the rushing water turned the wheels, which would in turn activate the gears of the mill.

Three different kinds of wheels were used in gristmills. The first kind were called overshot wheels. The radiuses of these wheels had buckets attached to them which filled with water; the weight of the full buckets caused the wheel to move. Most of these wheels had diameters of about 12 or 15 feet. But the largest of them measured about 36 feet in diameter. The decision on how large a wheel to build was made by estimating the water power available to drive it.

The second kind of wheel was the undershot wheel. It was much the same as the overshot, except the water flowed beneath it, propelling paddles that were attached to the radiuses. These wheels were smaller than the overshots and required less power to operate.

The final development in watered powered wheels for gristmills was the introduction of the iron turbine wheel. Water flowed to its axle and turned it from there. Although it was the smallest wheel, it provided the most power.

Although water wheels were a good way of harnessing energy, gristmills did have some problems. Mill dams were made of logs, mud, and wood, and they took a beating from the force of the water in spring and the frost and ice in fall and winter. Frequently, they were damaged and required costly repairs. The wheels themselves were sometimes protected by wooden shelters which shielded them from the ravages of the weather.

Another problem with water powered gristmills was that when the flow was weak, operations had to be suspended. And good sites, with an abundant water flow, were scarce. Some people attempted to solve this problem by building windmills instead of water powered mills. But it is hard to believe that the strength of the breeze was any more reliable than the flow of the water.

Comber

The **Tilbury West Agricultural Museum** is located just three miles south of Comber on Highway 77. It is housed in a former school and displays there focus on the local history and agricultural development.

There's also an **Antique Market and Crafts Sale** held on the third Sunday of each month at the Comber Agricultural Hall.

Cookstown

Cookstown, and the surrounding area is one of the busiest areas for shopping and dining in rural Ontario. There are many craft stores in the town. One of these stores is **Mostly Pottery** on Highway 89, just west of Highway 27. This store specializes in wheelthrown pottery and custom silver. All the items sold there are made on the premises. **The Village Craftsman** is located on Cookstown's main street in a building constructed in 1873. It carries supplies for making textiles as well as finished textile products including clothes, wall hangings, and puppets. The proprietors of the store also offer courses in textile making. **D.C.'s Antiques and Fine Furniture** is another interesting place to shop in Cookstown. Located on Highway 89, west of Highway 27, this shop has a large selection of antiques and fine furnishings. Auctions are held there every Sunday too. **The Towne Crossing** is also found on Highway 89, west of 27. It carries handcrafted gifts and decorating items.

The Chesnut Inn, a fine restaurant housed in a country home built in the 1800s, is situated next to the Towne Crossing. On summer afternoons, you can enjoy tea and cocktails on their outdoor patio. If you're interested in trying your own hand at some country cooking, you'll want to visit **Country Concession,** a store which sells country cooking utensils and gifts. They also have their own tea room. Another country dining spot is located in Gilford, east of Cookstown. The **Barkley Square Inn** creates an old world atmosphere around their cozy fireplace. It is near the corner of Highways 11 and 89 and specializes in European cuisine. South of Cookstown at Bond Head, you'll find the **Barclay House Craft Shop.** It is located on the Innisfil Beach Side Rd. and features quilted items, weaving, pottery, and clothes. It's open from Wednesday to Sunday during July and August, and on weekends the rest of the time between May and December. It seems there's a country dining spot in every direction from Cookstown. North on Highway 27 takes you to the **Village Inn** in Thornton. The restaurant is found in a home over 100 years old. There's also an adjoining antique shop to browse through. Last but not least, there's another restaurant worth visiting in Bradford, southeast of Cookstown. **The Quaint House** is found in a farm house built midway through the nineteenth century. This restaurant features home baking and cooking. It is located at the junction of Highways 11 and 88. A visit to **High Hopes Antiques** makes a trip to Bradford even more worthwhile. It is located 7 km south of Cookstown on RR2 in an old general store at the top of the hill. It has an assortment of glassware, metalware, fixtures, and a special collection of coin-operated machines.

Cornwall

The United Counties Museum in Cornwall was originally intended to be a blockhouse to protect the Canadian border and the Cornwall Canal, but a land dispute changed these plans, and it became a private home before becoming a museum. It features early nineteenth century household articles as well as some electrical equipment originally installed by Thomas Edison in the Canada Mill.

A couple of shops worth visiting in Cornwall are **The Chalet,** manufacturers and retailers of artistic free-form glass, and **Bernie's Fine Antique Furnishings and Collectibles** located at 223A McConnell.

Just east of Cornwall on Highway 2 is **La Seigneurie St. Laurent Dining Lounge.** This restaurant is found in a home built in 1828, overlooking the St. Lawrence.

There's a place near Lancaster, northeast of Cornwall that you'll want to stop at if you're in the mood for a little good food and exercise. **Gerbig's Farm Market,** just east of Lancaster on Highway 2 features raspberries, tomatoes, and beans. It's open daily from late June until mid-October.

Delhi

This town is located in the heart of Ontario's tobacco growing region. And the **Delhi Experimental Farm** is a good place to learn about the various aspects of tobacco production. Research on the subject is carried out on this farm. It is located west of Delhi, 5 km on Highway 3 and 1 km north on Schaefer Road. It's open year round from Monday to Friday.

North of Delhi on Highway 53 is a fine craft shop in Burford known as **The Chalet Boutique.** The shop features Mennonite quilts, pottery, weaving, dolls, and macrame. It is closed on Wednesdays.

Dorset

The **Leslie M. Frost Natural Resources Centre** at Dorset offers both live-in and day-use outdoor education programs. The programs are designed to educate both children and adult groups in various aspects of nature and conservation. Casual visitors are welcome and they can observe a variety of demonstrations. One of these demonstrations is of a working sawmill. Others concern geology, trail planning for outdoor activities, fur bearer management, and lake and stream management.

You can also look for gifts and crafts in the Dorset area at **The Log Cabin,** on Highway 117 on the way to Baysville.

Dresden

This town has a rather unusual claim to fame. It is the home of **Uncle Tom's Cabin Museum.** The Reverend Josiah Henson, a black American slave who inspired Harriet Beecher's famous novel, fled to Canada and took up residence in Dresden. It was there that he set up the British American Institute, a refuge and rehabilitation centre for other runaway slaves. The Institute developed into Canada's first vocational school. The museum is comprised of six buildings, including Henson's home.

Northwest of the nearby town of Wallaceburg on the St. Clair Parkway is the **Snyeview Farm Market.** This market is part of the Niagara fruit belt and offers customers the opportunity to harvest their own apples, strawberries, cherries, and corn, when they're in season.

Dundas

The **Dundas Craftsman** at 14 Cross St. handles the work of many local craftspeople, so there is a variety of craft items for sale. Choose from leatherwork, pottery, pine furniture, clothing, weaving, some musical instruments, batik, jewellery, and wooden toys. If you're a failed gardener yet enjoy the fruits of someone else's green thumb, you'll enjoy a visit to the **Ben Velduis Greenhouses.** Visitors are welcome at the greenhouses which feature cacti and other succulents.

Eganville

This town is famous for its fascinating caves. The **Bonnechere Caves** lie beneath a hill of limestone. Apparently they were formed by running water and twist through the rock as a result of this.

Geologists say that the limestone hill was the bottom of a tropical sea some 500 million years ago. Stalactites hanging from the roof of the caves are enhanced by colourful electric lights. One of the most fascinating aspects of the caves is the fossils of coral and sea creatures that are embedded in the rock. The caves are open to the public from May to October.

Elmira

Elmira still reflects Pennsylvania Dutch country culture in many ways. The best overall view of this influence is gained by taking the **Countryside Tour.** A representative of the Chamber of Commerce will accompany you and provide commentary as you see a buggy factory, the Mennonite Buggy Bridge, a blacksmith shop, and a covered bridge, the only remaining one in Ontario.

There are many good places to shop in Elmira. **Brox's Olde Town Village** is a shopping centre that combines the convenience of shopping at many stores under one roof, with country items in a country atmosphere. The Village includes several craft stores, a cheese store, flower and plant shops, a gift shop, a candy store, and an ice cream parlour.

One of the biggest and most interesting crafts practised extensively in the area is quilt making. You can find quilted items for sale as well as a quilt gallery at **The Sap Bucket.** This store is located in a 150 year old stone house, and also features other craft items, such as apple dolls, embroidered goods, homemade soap, and homemade tea balls. Another good store to know about in Elmira is **Richard's Dry Goods** at 3 Arthur St. S. This old fashioned store provides local quilt makers with an interesting selection of fabrics. So if you're inspired by the beautiful quilts you see in Elmira, this store is a good place to get supplies you can use to make your own.

There's a fascinating exhibition of a rather unique craft in Elmira at the **House of Dolls.** On display are historical dolls, antique dolls,

storybook dolls, and novelty dolls. The collection is exhibited in the home of the owner at 28 South St. in Elmira. Since it is in a private home, large groups and tours must be arranged in advance.

There's also a **Farmer's Market** on Saturday mornings in Elmira. It features many of the Mennonite specialties such as cheese, homemade butter and sausages, and fresh fruit and vegetables. The market is located on Church St.

Elora

Elora is a pretty village located at the Grand River Falls. Many craft shops line the main street and lead down to the breathtaking **Elora Gorge.** The Gorge is a limestone canyon with many waterfalls, rapids, and caves. Indian people in the area believed that spirits lived between the walls of the Gorge. There's a 300 acre park around the Gorge, so try to catch the view from the **Elora Mill Restaurant.** This restaurant is located in one of the few five storey gristmills still in existence. Up the street, **Cafe Flore** offers fine French food at reasonable prices, served on locally made pottery.

Elora is quite a town for crafts. There are several pottery shops operating there including **Peter and Nancy's Pottery.** Their shop is located in a renovated church that was built in 1877. They carry some stained glass items as well as pottery. Outside of town, on the way to Salem, is **Gordon's Pottery.** This shop specializes in "everything to furnish a kitchen in pottery." The **Magic Mountain Trading Company,** at 48 Mill St., features crafts, as well as clothing and art from Latin America. **The Easel,** at 43 Mill St. W., includes wood and stone carvings, rock paintings, leather paintings, and aluminum etchings in their collection of goods. **Copper Craft by Jellybean Ltd.** at 40 Mill Road features brass and copper miniatures, antique reproductions, and copper cookware. **The Green Owl** at 42 Mill St. W. features Canadian crafts including pottery, weaving, jewellery, and hand-loomed ensembles. **The Silver Shop** at 123 Metcalfe sells jewellery in gold and silver. A good place to explore for antiques would be the **By George Antique and Flea Market.** It's open every day but Mondays and is located on the Elora-Guelph Road.

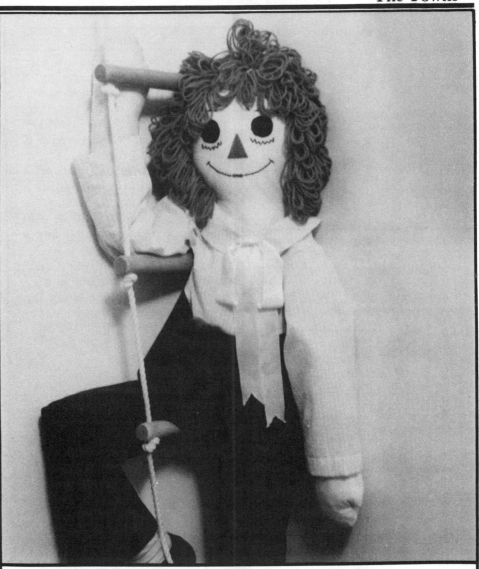

Country candy

If all those homemade candies in country stores get your mouth watering and your sweet tooth aching, try this recipe when you get home.

Old-Style Chocolate Fudge

Boil together 1 cup brown sugar, 1 cup white sugar, 1 and a half squares bittersweet chocolate, 1 tablespoon butter, and half a cup milk. Add 1 teaspoon vanilla. Beat the mixture with a wooden spoon until creamy. Spread it on a buttered platter, and when cool, cut into pieces.

The Towns

There's a farm produce outlet near Elora called **Glenmar Farms** where you can harvest your own strawberries, raspberries, and beans It's open Tuesdays, Thursdays, and weekends. To get there, take Highway 6 north from Guelph to Elora Road, follow the road for 8 km, and watch for signs on the left hand side.

Erin

Erin is a good place to shop for antiques and crafts. **The Farmhouse Pottery** has hand-thrown stoneware and porcelain. It is located on RR2 and is open daily. **The Village Craft Shop** is found at 120 Main St. in Erin, and specializes in hand crafts, plants, flowers, prints, and frames. It's open Monday through Saturday. **The Woodbin,** is located at 194 Main St. and features handcrafted furniture, pottery, curios, and woven goods. **The Robin's Nest,** specializing in wallhangings, is at 192 Main St. **Swampman's Antiques** operates out of 30 Main St., and features pine, primitives, unusual collectibles, and refinishing supplies for do-it-yourselfers.

Flesherton

Flesherton has a reputation for being a good place to look for antiques. **Marples Antiques and Refinishing,** or **Penny's Flea Market** might be good starting points for an antique hunting trip.

The South Grey Museum and Historical Library will show you how your found treasures were once used. The museum is open daily during July and August, and on weekends in the early summer and fall.

Beaver Valley Crafts is also found in Flesherton.

Gananoque

Gananoque is an especially nice place to be during the summer. It's located near the Thousand Islands area of the St. Lawrence River and you can take **Boat Cruises** through the islands from there between mid-May and mid-October.

A good place for family entertainment in Gananoque is **The Tinker's Dam** on King St. West. It includes an outdoor craft market, a puppet theatre, and a European Style cafe.

Two good restaurants in the city are the **Golden Apple Inn** on King St. E., and the **Athlone Motor Inn Dining Lounge** on King St. W. The Athlone is located in a Victorian style home built in 1874 and is refurnished to that period. The Golden Apple is housed in a farmhouse built in the early 1800s and is furnished with antiques. Visitors can dine in the house by the fireplace, or under the apple boughs of the orchard in summer.

Goderich

Goderich is a pretty town located on the east side of Lake Huron. At the centre of the city is the **Huron Historical Gaol,** an unusual eight-sided building. It was built in 1839-1840 and is one of the few remaining examples of early prison architecture. The cell blocks radiate from a central stairwell. The gaoler's residence is attached to the gaol and is restored to the period around the turn of the century. The gaol is open daily from Victoria Day to Labour Day and after that, on weekends until the end of October. It's located on Victoria St. Another site of historical interest in Goderich is the **Huron County Pioneer Museum** at 110 North St. One of the highlights of this museum is a series of displays which trace the development of transportation methods from the horse to the tractor to the locomotive. Other exhibits relate to the history of milling in Ontario.

This museum is open daily from April through October (except for Sundays in April).

You'll probably learn a little more about milling in Ontario if you go to the **Benmiller Inn** for a meal. This restaurant is located in a 125 year old mill situated 3 km off Highway 8.

North of Goderich in Port Albert, there's a place where you'll see an abundance of interesting fish. The **Port Albert Fishway** gives migratory rainbow trout a way to pass over a natural rock obstruction. The time to visit is during the spring and fall spawning runs.

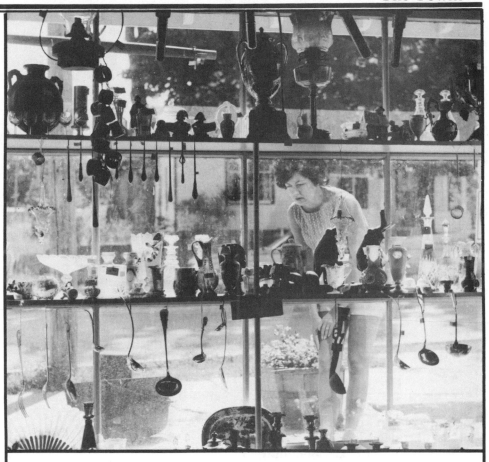

Gravenhurst

One usually thinks of a big city as the place for a night on the town. But Gravenhurst is proof that nightlife is alive in small towns too. What could be more pleasant than gliding along a lake on a boat with a good band providing the entertainment? **Music on the Barge** is just that, a band concert held every Sunday evening on a barge which cruises Gull Lake. Another suggestion for an evening of entertainment is to attend one of the plays offered by **Muskoka Summer Theatre.** Performances are given Monday to Saturday in the Gravenhurst Opera House during July and August.

An interesting daytime outing in Gravenhurst would be a trip to the **Bethune Memorial House.** The house is the former home of the world famous Canadian doctor, Norman Bethune, who is known for his work in China. It has been restored to the time of Bethune's birth (1890) and there's a display which portrays his life through quotes and pictures.

Children would enjoy a visit to **Corbette's Zooette,** located at the southern entrance to Gravenhurst. It contains 70 different kinds of animals and birds in a park-like setting.

Guelph

It's not unusual to tell the time of year by flowers. When they bloom, it's spring. But in this town, flowers tell the time of day! Guelph is the home of a **Mechanical Floral Clock,** which is 47 feet in diameter and contains thousands of flowers. You can find out the time for yourself in Riverside Park.

The **Kortright Waterfowl Park** is also a place worth visiting in the Guelph area. This is a wildlife area and waterfowl research centre with over 70 different species. You can see ducks, swans, geese, and other wild birds in their natural surroundings. It's located on Kortright Rd., 4 km west of Highway 6 on the Speed River. It's open daily, year round.

Haliburton

This small village is located in the midst of the hundreds of beautiful lakes that dot the Haliburton Highlands. One of the original pioneer homes in the area is now part of the **Haliburton Highlands Pioneer Museum.** The home has been restored and includes many of the furnishings that one would find in a house around the 1880 period. The museum also features a collection of Canadian china and glassware, early photographs from the area, and some tools and implements used for lumbering, agriculture, and trapping. It's open from mid-June to Thanksgiving on weekend afternoons, as well as every afternoon during July and August.

If you're hoping to take a piece of the past home with you, why not check out some of the antique stores in Haliburton? There's **Echoes of Yesterday,** and **Paulette's Antiques** and Gifts.

If it's crafts you're interested in, there's something for you too. **The Nuthatch,** on Kashaga Dr., off Highway 121, specializes in weaving, crocheting, knitting, leatherwork, ceramic tile plaques, and dishes.

Hall's Lake

Hall's Lake has one of the most unique museums in Ontario. **The Kanawa International Museum of Canoes, Kayaks, and Rowing Craft** is sure to interest any outdoorsman. It's found adjacent to Kandalore Camp off Highway 35.

Hamilton

This city is known for its cold, hard steel but it also features some beautiful, delicate plants and flowers. The **Royal Botanical Gardens** in Hamilton covers 2000 acres of land and includes floral displays, natural parkland, an arboretum, and a wildlife sanctuary, whose trails lead through areas of water, marshland, and wooded ravines.

Dundurn Castle is another attraction in this city. It is a 36 room, nineteenth century mansion that has been restored to that time period. It was the home of Sir Allan Napier MacNab, who was Prime Minister of the United Provinces of Canada from 1854 to 1856. Other aspects of the Castle are the Cockpit Theatre, which presents special children's entertainment during the summer, concerts in the courtyard, which are also given in summer, the MacNab Arms Restaurant, and a sound and light presentation which is also given in the summer.

An interesting part of the city of Hamilton is **Hess Village.** This is an area where old homes have been restored and now serve as specialty shops, galleries, and restaurants. It

is located in the area of Hess and George Streets. One of the restaurants in the village is the **Hess House,** housed in a mansion constructed around the turn of the century. Lunch is served on the outdoor patio in the summer.

A craft store in Hamilton that you might want to visit is the **Canvas Gallery Craft Boutique** at 21 Augusta St. It features blown glass, wall hangings, batik, ceramics, and many other items. And if you're in Hamilton on a Sunday, you should visit the **East Gate Square Flea Market.**

There's also a **Farmer's Market** in Hamilton. Fruit, flowers, and vegetables are the standard market fare. It's located at the Market Square at St. James North and York Sts. It's open year round on Tuesdays, Thursdays, and Saturdays.

Hillsburgh

The **Hillsburgh Farm Conservation Area** is one place where you can learn more about something that is often taken for granted: agriculture. It features agricultural demonstrations and old fashioned farm equipment that was handmade by pioneers.

Enjoy the fruits of agriculture with a visit to the **Welcome-In Restaurant.** It specializes in home cooked meals and also carries a selection of gifts, antiques, and collectibles.

Another shop you'll enjoy in Hillsburgh is the **Country Road Craft Gallery** at 113 Main St. This store features original designs in stained glass, ceramic jewellery, handthrown pottery, and other crafts. It's open every day including weekend afternoons. Just west of Hillsburgh in Orton is another antique craft shop. **Vera B** sells dolls, miniatures, dollhouses, antiques, and collectibles. It's found on Main St. and is open

afternoons, every day but Thursday.

Heidelberg

The German influence in southern Ontario is very much in evidence in some of the stores and restaurants of Heidelberg. The **Country Store** specializes in homemade pork sausage and summer sausage. And the **Olde Heidelberg House** restaurant is famous for its German cuisine.

Huntsville

Muskoka Pioneer Village alone makes a trip to Huntsville worthwhile. A knowledgable staff dressed in period costumes gives daily demonstrations of bread, butter, and ice cream making. They also show how candle-dipping and blacksmithing were done. A horse-drawn wagon will take you on a tour of the village so you can see the general store, schoolhouse, sawmill, blacksmith shop, church, and pioneer homes. There's also a museum where you can view pioneer and Indian artifacts. The village is open daily from June to September, and on weekends from September to Thanksgiving.

If you're in Huntsville during the winter, you should try the ski hill at **Timberlost Lodge.** And if you work up an appetite you could have a meal at the **House Bavaria** on Britannia Road, east of Muskoka Road 2. The building was once an early Canadian schoolhouse.

There's also a fine craft shop east of Huntsville at Dwight. **The Palmer House** is a century old home which now features articles made by the Mennonites. These items include their famous quilts, place mats, cushions, and rugs. The store sells many other crafts in addition to these, including weaving, ceramics, metalwork, and leatherwork. The shop is open daily from mid-June to mid-October, and on weekends only from mid-May to mid-June.

Huttonville

Huttonville is close enough to Toronto that residents of that city can get a taste of the country without too much travelling. If you'd like to pick up some fresh produce you should look for **Al Ferri's Farm.** From September until frost you can get apples, cider, honey, tomatoes, pears, and potatoes. It's open 7 days a week.

And while you're in this neck of the woods, you can take advantage of the fine meals served at the **Someplace Else Country Tavern and Restaurant.** This restaurant is located in an old loyalist home on Mississauga Road.

Ingersoll

Ingersoll is a name associated with cheese in the minds of many. And with just cause, for it is the site of the first cheese factory in Canada as well as a **Cheese Factory Museum.** The museum is a replica of a cheese factory circa 1860 and contains antique cheese making tools and machinery. It's open daily in July and August, and on weekend afternoons from May to September.

Curds and whey

For some time now, man has known that the moon is made of green cheese. But until now, few of us knew what the cheese was made of.

Green food colouring aside, cheddar cheese is made from whole milk. The first step in the process of making cheese is adding a bacterial culture to the milk that converts milk sugar to lactic acid. The resulting solution is heated to 30°C and stirred in a large vat. If artificial colouring is used, it is added at this stage. Generally, mild cheddar is orange while sharp cheddar is a natural, creamy white colour. Next, a coagulant is added to solidify the mixture.

At this stage, one has a solid curd which is cut into small cubes to be heated and stirred. When the curd is firm, the liquid (whey) is drained off and the curd is cut into loaf shaped pieces and turned periodically so it becomes smooth and matted. It is then shredded into thin strips, salted, and placed into molds where it is pressed into blocks or rounds. After many hours of pressure to shape the cheese the molded pieces are dipped in wax and subsequently packaged in plastic to prevent weight loss and mold developing.

Once packaged, cheddar is allowed to ripen under controlled temperature and humidity. The humidity is not more than 60 percent and the temperature should be close to 2°C. Mild cheddar is aged for two or three months, medium flavoured cheddar is aged for four to five months, and old or sharp cheddar is aged for at least nine months and sometimes more.

Cheese tends to dry out if it is not wrapped tightly in plastic and refrigerated. However, if it does dry out, it can still be grated and used in cooking.

Cheese can be frozen and kept for up to three months. It should be cut into pieces about one inch thick and wrapped tightly, first in plastic, and then in aluminum foil. When you are ready to use it, it's best to thaw it out gradually, moving it from the freezer to the refrigerator.

Even if cheese develops mold on the surface, it needn't be thrown out. The mold can be cut off or scraped away, leaving the rest of the piece suitable for eating.

Cheese is essentially a concentrated form of milk which is a good source of protein. One and a half ounces of cheese provides nearly half the amount of calcium recommended for an adult each day. It is also estimated that a two ounce portion of cheese is equivalent to a serving of meat. And just because it's good for you doesn't mean that people aren't eating it. Two thirds of all the cheese consumed in Canada is Canadian cheddar.

Iroquois Falls

This town is in the heart of pulp and paper country. If you're interested in finding out a little more about the industry, you can take **The Pulp and Paper Path.** This is a seven hour guided tour of the various steps in a modern logging operation. The tour covers everything from tree planting to the manufacture of newsprint. A school bus takes you around the various sites and stops frequently so you can get out and have a closer look at some of the woodland operations. The tour leaves on weekday mornings, except Monday, during July and August, from the **Iroquois Falls Museum.** The museum is housed in an old railway station on Cambridge St. It contains pioneer tools, housewares, and family treasures that serve to illustrate the history of Ontario's north. This museum is open during July and August.

Jordan

This small town is probably best known for the wine that is made there. And you can see an old fashioned fruit press for making wine on display at the **Jordan Historical Museum of the Twenty.** The museum is a three-building complex which includes a stone schoolhouse, a pioneer home, and the Vintage House. It's open daily in the afternoons from early May to late October.

Another interesting place to visit in the Jordan area is the **Ball's Falls Conservation Area.** There's also a museum located there. It features a 165 year old gristmill, log cabins, an apple drying shed, a lime kiln, a blacksmith shop, and a church.

One of the natural highlights of the area is the waterfalls found there. The highest waterfall is about a 27 metre drop. The Conservation Area is open from Victoria Day to Labour Day.

Jordan may also be a good place to look for bargains. The **Jordan Valley Flea Market** is open every Sunday.

Keene

A visit to Keene is a good opportunity to have a glimpse of pioneer life in Ontario. Your first stop should be **Century Village.** This village is comprised of 14 restored buildings including a store, shingle mill, inn, and cider barn. Pioneer activities and arts and crafts take place there all summer long. The village is open daily during July and August, and on weekends only the rest of the time between Victoria Day and Thanksgiving.

Another aspect of pioneer life in Keene is **The Lang Gristmill and the Hope Sawmill.** Both nineteenth century, water-powered mills are still in working order today. The mills are open daily during July and August, and on weekends only during May, June, September, and October.

Kenora

Located on the north shore of Lake of the Woods, Kenora is situated in the heart of some beautiful, unspoiled wilderness country. To get a good look at some of this country, why not take a tour of the islands in the Lake of the Woods? **Lake Cruises** tour the area for two hours every day from late May to September.

Another place to visit in Kenora is the **Lake of the Woods Museum.** This museum includes a collection of Indian and pioneer artifacts and a good mineralogical exhibit. It's situated on Water St. and it's open year round. The museum is open daily except from October through April when it's closed on Saturdays and Sundays.

If you're looking for antiques in Kenora, you should visit the **Blue Heron Gift and Antique Shop.** It features furniture, crafts, and jewellery among other things.

Kingston

Kingston is a city that is steeped in military and naval history. Located at the mouth of the St. Lawrence River, the city is the site of **Old Fort Henry,** once a military stronghold in Upper Canada. Now it houses a large collection of arms and equipment. Daily features of the fort are a nineteenth century infantry drill, exhibitions by a fife and drum band, and artillery salutes with a cannon. Demonstrations are also given in leather-working, tailoring, and baking. The Fort is open daily from mid-May until mid-October.

Another interesting historical site is the **Kingston Marine Museum.** It features a collection of items salvaged from shipwrecks in the area, as well as small boats and marine accessories. The museum is located on Lower Union St. and is also open from mid-May to mid-October. Maybe the museum will interest you enough that you decide to take one of the **Thousand Islands Cruises** that tour the islands of the St. Lawrence in the Kingston area. Boats leave from a dock 8 km east of Fort Henry on Highway 2. Cruises are offered from mid-May until late September.

A good place to eat in Kingston is the **Firehall Restaurant.** This building has been restored to how it looked in 1840. The dining room has a rustic look to it with a working fireplace, stone and brick walls, and a small, intimate bar. The restaurant is situated at 251 Ontario St.

There are also some interesting shops in Kingston. One craft store in the area exhibits work as well as sells it. **The Canadian Shop of Kingston and Gallery of Fine Canadian Crafts** at 219 Princess St. features a wide variety of craft items for sale and on display. **Silverstone Antiques** is another shop you should visit in the Kingston area. It's located on RR8, 2 km north of Highway 401. This dealer features Canadiana, Victorian furniture, china, glassware, silver, and other items.

Kingsville

The Jack Miner Bird Sanctuary is Kingsville's most famous attraction. The centre attracts visitors from all over, especially during the migration seasons of fall and spring. March and early April, and October and early November, are the best months for observing the birds.

The **Southwestern Ontario Heritage Village** is also located in Kingsville. It consists of eight historic buildings and a transportation history museum. The museum features a collection of about 50 vintage vehicles. The other buildings in the village include a railway station and an old fashioned school-house.

Kirkfield

Kirkfield is the site of the **MacKenzie Historic Home.** The home was built in 1877 and Sir William MacKenzie, co-founder of the Canadian northern railway lived there. Some of the 40 rooms in this mansion are devoted to the railway and its history. The home can be found on Highway 48 and is open daily, year round. The home also has a dining area known as the **Gatehouse Restaurant.** This Victorian style room is open for lunches. During the summer, customers can eat outdoors on the patio.

Another spot worth visiting in Kirkfield is **LKJ Antiques and Used Articles.**

Kirkland Lake

This town is famous because of the many professional hockey players who grew up here. But there's more to the town than that. The **Museum of Northern History** traces the development of mining in Ontario's north and includes displays of old mining equipment. It also features Indian and Inuit artifacts. Some of the companies in the area offer **Mine Tours,** and the Museum has information about them.

Another aspect of the northern part of Ontario is the wildlife. A good place to observe a large number of animals is **Herman's Wildlife Park** at the junction of Highways 11 and 112, 25 km south of town. The park features many animals from northern habitats including buffalo, caribou, reindeer, arctic horned owls, fishers, foxes, and martens.

If you want to pick up a souvenir of the area, you can visit **The Craft Cupboard** on Highway 66. It features handcrafted souvenirs including Indian crafts, rock jewellery, quilts, and hooked rugs.

Kitchener

You can see many remnants of the pioneer lifestyle at the **Doon Pioneer Village,** just southeast of Kitchener. You'll see wagons, steam fire engines, carpet looms, old quilts, and Indian artifacts. The 60 acre complex includes several reconstructed buildings including a church, a sawmill, a blacksmith's shop, and a general store. It's open from May to October in the afternoons, from Tuesday to Saturday.

There are also some good, old fashioned places to shop in Kitchener. You can't get much more old fashioned than buying food directly from the farmer and that's exactly what you do at the

Kitchener Farmer's Market. This market is said to be the largest and oldest in Ontario. It features many special items made by the Mennonites of the area including dutch apple pie, shoofly pie, jams and jellies, apple butter, handmade knives, and various crafts. It's located in the market square at Frederick and Duke Sts. and is open year round on Saturdays, and also on Wednesdays from May to December. Another great place to shop is the **Highway Market** at 2722 King St. E. You'll find such rare items as snuff, chewing tobacco, corn brooms, kerosene, oil lamps, and cast iron pots here. There's another country style store to the south of Kitchener in Preston. **Myth and Magic**, at 903 King St. E. sells fresh local produce, books, plants, jewellery, soaps, jams, pottery, and fruit and nuts. Another old store is found to the south of Kitchener in New Dundee. **The Emporium** is a Victorian store that features gifts, antiques, and country confections.

Kleinburg

It's just a short hop from Toronto to Kleinburg where you can view the famous **McMichael Canadian Collection** of paintings. The gallery is located in a quiet, wooded area and features many works by Group of Seven artists. It also includes works by Indian and Inuit artists. The gallery is open year round, every day except Mondays.

While in Kleinburg you can enjoy a meal at **The Doctor's House and Livery.** This 100 year old home serves Canadian dishes of the 1800s. There's also a gift shop on the premises, located at Nashville Rd. and Islington Ave.

Lakefield

If you enjoy a little exploring, you'll appreciate the **Warsaw Caves** in Lakefield. These limestone tunnels are over 90 metres underground so you'd better bring a flashlight!

You may also want to do some shopping because Lakefield is a good place to buy crafts and cheddar cheese. It is also a good place for antiques. **Bowman Furniture and Antiques** would be an excellent place to start.

If you're looking for a place to eat in the area, a short trip north to Young's Point will take you to the **Old Bridge Inn.** It was originally built in 1904 as a stopover for the horse and buggy trade. Now it's a restaurant with early Canadian decor.

Leamington

The most southerly tip of the Canadian mainland is found at **Point Pelee National Park** near Leamington. The park includes nature trails, a tour train, and beaches. Nature buffs will appreciate the boardwalk through the marsh with observation towers from which you can view the birds and wildlife.

If hiking through the park makes you hungry you can look for **Thirteen Russell** at the junction of Highways 3 and 77. This restaurant is located in a turn of the century home which is stocked with antique furniture.

If you go west on Highway 3 to Ruthven, you should not miss a trip through the tropics. **Colasanti's Cactus and Tropical Greenhouses** invites visitors to browse through the plants, displays of tropical birds, and a waterfall with pools and streams for fish.

Lindsay

This pleasant town is found on the shores of the Scugog River on the Trent Canal System. One of its most renowned summer attractions is the **Academy Theatre,** which specializes in comedies. Performances are held Tuesdays through Saturdays from July to Labour Day.

The **Victoria County Historical Museum** is also located in Lindsay. It includes displays which focus on the history of the area. Exhibits of Canadian glass and oil lamps, as well as an apothecary shop, a toy store, a general store, and a doctor's office await your viewing. The museum also has an agricultural display and a log cabin. It's open from Victoria Day to Labour Day, Tuesday to Sunday afternoons.

You'll find some interesting craft items for sale at **Burridge's Century House** on RR6 at Pleasant Point. It features furniture, quilts, glass, china, crocks, paintings, and prints.

If you're an antique buff, there's a shop in Lindsay you'll want to visit. **Jackson's Antiques** features Victorian furniture, glass and china, lamp parts, and lampshades. It's located at 133 Williams N. and is open evenings and weekends.

Northeast of Lindsay near Dunsford, you'll find **The Robertson 1867 Farm.** There, you'll be able to pick your own strawberries, raspberries, beans, tomatoes, or sweet corn, depending on what's in season.

Vacation farms

If you're a parent who continually reminds your children of how tough but good it was to live on a farm, you can back up your claims by taking them to an Ontario Vacation Farm.

Ontario Vacation Farms are geared towards family holidays, however some farms do offer accommodation for adults and children on their own. These farm holidays are part of a program sponsored by the Ontario Ministry of Agriculture and Food. Many of the farms welcome visitors at any time of year for a weekend, a week, or an extended holiday.

There are a number of interesting kinds of farms to choose from. And once you're there you can join in on the farm chores to clear the cobwebs out of your head, or just sit back and enjoy the country atmosphere. The opportunity to learn about farming, see farm animals, and just get away from it all is especially good for children. There are many things that children can learn on one of these trips that won't be taught in school.

One of the nicest things about this kind of holiday is that you'll get to know some friendly country people. Usually, the farmers and their families will take time out to spend some time with you and tell you what you can see and do in the area.

Another great thing about these holidays is that staying on the farm can be combined with any number of other outdoor activities. With experts on the surrounding areas close at hand, you'll easily find the best spots for hiking, fishing, swimming, cross-country skiing, or any other recreational pasttime. You may also want to visit nearby towns where you can poke around at antique stores and flea markets.

There are varying kinds of accommodation offered at these farms. Some have camping facilities while others offer private housekeeping units or rooms in farmhouses. Often, you can arrange to join the farmer's family for meals. A Vacation Farm differs from a hotel or a resort in many ways. As well as taking advantage of all the opportunities offered you, it is important that you co-operate with any house rules there may be.

There are about 30 Vacation Farms operating in Ontario and their prices are very reasonable. You'll also find that some of them are not located too far from cities, and that makes them even more affordable.

For a different, interesting vacation, try an Ontario Vacation Farm: for more information write the Ontario Vacation Farm Association or the Ontario Ministry of Agriculture and Food. The Association's address is RR2, Erin, Ontario, N0B 1T0 and the Ministry is located at 801 Bay Street in Toronto.

Linwood

Shopping in old fashioned country stores is a pleasure that one rarely gets to enjoy anymore — except in Linwood. **Schnurr's Grocery** was established in 1860 but it still provides a full range of groceries and specializes in home baked goods. The **Linwood General Store** is in the same league. It specializes in homemade sausage and fresh meats, but sells yard goods and clothing as well.

London

Touring factories is always an interesting prospect but somehow touring a brewery is even more exciting. **The Pioneer Brewery** in London shows visitors exactly how the suds were made by John Labatt in 1854. Inside, the building is filled with old brewing equipment from that time and fixtures and furnishings to match. Swinging tin lanterns shine down on wooden fermenters and cooling pans.

While you may not find hops and barley at the **Covent Garden Market,** you'll probably find just about everything else in the way of food. This farmer's market is found off Market Lane in downtown London and you'll find produce, cheeses, baked goods, delicatessen meats, imported foods, and even some crafts there. There are also many retail stores that sell craft items in London. One of them is **The Canadian Craftsman** at 231 Wellington St. It features woodwork, pottery, weaving, batik, Indian and Inuit art, and many other craft items. Another craft outlet is **The Gallery Shop** at 305 Queens Ave. It carries blown glass, jewellery, ceramics, weaving, and batik.

If you're interested in seeing demonstrations of pioneer crafts, you'll want to visit **Fanshawe Park and Pioneer Village.** This is a conservation area that includes a

village where old fashioned craft making takes place. It's located just east of the city off Clarke Road.

London seems to offer something for everyone, including the antique buff. One place to visit is **Heritage Shop Antiques** at 389 Talbot St. It specializes in furniture, china, rugs, wicker, and bamboo. Another antique shop is in nearby Lambeth. **Trembley's Antiques** on RR2 specializes in glass, Canadiana furniture, and leaded stained glass. If you have the patience to browse for antiques you'll be interested in the **Four City Flea Market,** held on Sunday afternoons every month except September. It's held in the Special Events Building at the Western Fairgrounds.

There are also some good pick-your-own produce outlets and farmer's markets in the London area. **Wood Lynn Farms Ltd.** at 502 Springbank Drive and 324 Commissioners Road (West London) specialize in fresh meat and produce as well as pick-your-own apples and cherries. South of London, on Talbot Road, just north of the Lambeth traffic light is the **Applegate Orchard and Fruit Market.** It specializes in fruit baskets and pick-your-own apples, pears, beans, and tomatoes.

Manitoulin Island

Meldrum Bay, is located on the western tip of Manitoulin Island. And because of that simple geographic fact, it's the home of the **Mississaugi Strait Lighthouse.** The lighthouse was built in 1874 and has been restored with the furnishings of that time. Toronto may have Ontario's only CN Tower but the view of the strait from this lighthouse is also a joy to behold. The lighthouse is open daily from July 1 to early September all day long. From mid-May to July 1 and from mid-September to mid-October it's open in the afternoons.

The **Nat Shed Museum** in Meldrum Bay features displays of artifacts used by pioneer fishermen and farmers. It's open from July 1 to early September in the afternoons and evenings.

At the northeast tip of Manitoulin Island in a town called Little Current, there's the **Little Current-Howland Centennial Museum.** This museum includes several two-storey log houses, a log granary, a blacksmith shop, and an agricultural shop too.

Mattawa

You can enjoy the northern Ontario wilderness on a trip to Mattawa. Just 13 km west of town on Highway 17, you'll find the **Voyageur Canoe Exhibit.** One of the highlights of this exhibit is a 38 foot birchbark canoe, a replica of one used by the North West Fur Company in about 1800. There's also an explorer's exhibit. The exhibit is part of Samuel de Champlain Park, which offers conducted hiking or moonlight canoe trips for the adventurous. It also offers film and slide programs including a special one for children.

Maynooth

There are a couple of craft shops that will interest you in Maynooth. **The Madawaska Art Shop** sells Canadian and imported handicrafts as well as original paintings and prints. One of their specialties is unique, sculptured candles. **The Silver Owl Studio** on RR1 is a former boarding house and hotel that was built in 1907. Now, it has been renovated to house a jewellery studio, an arts and crafts shop, and a family residence.

Melbourne

Melbourne is the home of the **Ska-Nah-Doht Indian Village.** This name translates to mean "a village starts again," and that is exactly the case. Ska-Nah-Doht is a fully reconstructed Indian village situated on Highway 2 in the Longwoods Conservation area. The spirit of the settlement is maintained by the tilling of an Indian garden each year. Indian corn and squash are planted in mounds around burnt tree stumps as they were hundreds of years ago. And the earth is tilled with tools made of bones and shells. Some of the buildings in the village are longhouses, a sweatlodge, buildings for drying meat and fish, a council house, and a medicine man's building. Each building contains pioneer artifacts from the 1800s, Indian artifacts and crafts, and paintings. The museum is located on Highway 68 at the village of Sheguiandah. It's open daily from May to October. Little Current also has the **Gore Bay Museum.** It's located behind the court house on Main St. in what used to be the town jail. Now the rooms there contain furniture and other possessions of the Island's pioneers and relics from old shipwrecks. It's open daily from June to August.

Midland

Midland reflects the history of the Huron Indians in the area. **Sainte Marie Among the Hurons** is probably the best known historical site. This seventeenth century Jesuit community served as a mission for priests ministering to the Indian people. The community is fully restored and includes a longhouse, workshops, a church, and a hospital. Craftsmen provide demonstrations, utilizing the technology of that time. It's open from Victoria Day until Thanksgiving.

The **Huron Indian Village** goes back a little further in history. It is a reconstruction of a typical Indian village prior to contact with people of European origins. Tour the buildings in the Village and observe the remains of a by-gone lifestyle. You'll learn even more about Huron culture by watching a film shown there. The Village is located at the east end of Little Lake Park and is open from May to December.

The **Huronia Museum** features Huron artifacts found on archeological digs in the area. It also includes some pioneer items such as pottery, glassware, and maps. There is also a collection of Canadian paintings, including works by the Group of Seven. This museum is also open from Victoria Day to Thanksgiving.

One attraction of the Midland area that does not rely on history is the **Wye Marsh Wildlife Centre.** You can really explore the area on trails, a boardwalk over the marsh, an observation tower, and even an underwater window. Inside the centre, naturalists are available to provide you with information about wildlife and answer your questions. They also lead nature walks. There's also a theatre and display hall inside the Centre. It too, is open from Victoria Day until Thanksgiving.

There's a large craft dealer in Midland that you'll want to visit. **The Artisan's Market Place** at 345 King St. includes the work of over 100 local craftspeople, so you can imagine the wide variety of crafts awaiting you there. Another place to buy crafts in Midland is at **Castle Village Shops.** You can get pine, wicker ware, lamps, brass, cast iron, copper, glass, crystal, and china. It's located on Balm Beach Rd. and is open daily.

If you're an optimist who's interested in antiques, there's a shop for you in Midland. It's called **Wishes Come True** and it carries stoneware, brass, china, glass, oil lamps, and Canadiana. It's located at 82 Eighth St.

Milton

There's lots to see and do in Milton, and it's close enough to Toronto that it would make a nice day-trip. The **Halton Regional Museum** houses one of the more unusual collections found in pioneer museums — their collection of lighting includes everything from rush lights to Coleman lamps.

If you're interested in the history of farming in Ontario, a visit to the **Ontario Agricultural Museum** would be in order. Different lots on the museum grounds depict farming activities and equipment from various eras. It's open daily during the summer, and from Monday to Friday the rest of the year.

A visit to the **Mountsberg Wildlife Centre** is an interesting and educational experience. Demonstrations of wilderness activities, and special events, are held regularly. The Centre is located west of Campbellville, off the Campbellville Rd.

There's an old fashioned store in Campbellville that has quite a bit to offer. It's called the **Campbellville Emporium** and it has three floors for you to browse through. The basement is full of antiques, the main floor has grocery items, and the top floor features gourmet foods. All things considered, it's a super place to buy what you need for a picnic lunch that you can eat in the park across the street.

There are several places in the Milton area where you can harvest your own produce. **Chudleigh's Apple Farm** on Highway 25, north of Highway 401, is open for picking your own during September and October. There's also a market there that is open from September to

December. This market specializes in homemade pies, fresh cider, apples, and sweet corn. **Braeside Farm** is open during July for harvesting your own raspberries and cherries. It's located south of Highway 401, 3 concessions west of Highway 25 on the Bell School Rd. Line, 1 km north of Derry Rd.

There's a restaurant in Milton that you might enjoy. **Harrop of Milton** is located in a century-old Georgian House that serves fine, English food. It's located at 345 Steeles Ave. E.

Morrisburg

This town is undoubtedly best known for the settlement found just 12 km east of it. **Upper Canada Village** is a series of 40 reconstructed pioneer buildings that authentically capture a pre-Confederation spirit. Pioneer activities such as blacksmithing, and working in a woolen mill and sawmill still take place, explained by guides in period costume. It's open daily from mid-May to mid-October.

Just a little further east of Morrisburg is a **Wildfowl Sanctuary.** It is 15 km east of town off Highway 2. During the spring and fall, it is an excellent place to observe the thousands of Canada geese that migrate south. You can keep an eye open for other wildlife as well while you wander through the sanctuary's 7 km of nature trails. If domesticated animals are more your thing, you can visit a **Riding Corral,** located about 10 km east of Morrisburg. They feature riding through woodlots and open fields.

Mount Hope

Antique browsers will find Mount Hope a good place to scrounge around on Sundays. Both the **Old Mill Antique Market** at 20 Airport Road and the **Flea Market** on Highway 6 do business on that day.

Niagara Falls

One thing that children are sure to enjoy in this city is **Marineland and Game Farm.** It features a dolphin, sea lion, and whale show, as well as animals from all over the world in a park-like setting.

A craft store that you will enjoy is **Peterson Woodcraft,** located at 8198 Curmington Square, Chippewa Town Hall. This store sells individually handcrafted carvings and wall plaques which feature many birds and animals. The **Long-Ago Shoppe** is a good place to look for fine, restored antique furniture. It's located at 5062 Drummond St.

The **Old Stone Inn** at 5425 Robinson St. is a nice, quiet restaurant amidst a jumble of tourist boutiques. It was built in 1904 as a flour mill but now it is decorated with exposed trusses, oak tables, Windsor chairs, and Victorian love seats. The restaurant features fine Canadian cuisine.

Niagara-On-the-Lake

This town is renowned for its **Shaw Festival** which features the plays of George Bernard Shaw and his contemporaries each summer, from May to September. But Niagara-On-the-Lake has much to offer beyond that.

The Niagara Apothecary at 5 Queen St. is a restored 1866 pharmacy, complete with wood furnishings of the time and original glass and ceramic ware. It's open from early May to early September.

The **Niagara Fire Museum** on King St. includes displays of firefighting equipment up to 140 years old. One of the most interesting items on display is the "mankiller," a water pump powered by 12 men. This unique museum is open from June to September.

There are a number of fine, country-style restaurants in Niagara-On-the-Lake. One of the premiere places is **The Pillar and Post Inn,** at King and John Sts. It is housed in a refurnished building that was built as a cannery in the early 1900s. The building also houses an arts and crafts shop that features pottery, textiles, batik, and jewellery. Another fine dining spot is the **Prince of Wales Hotel.** The building it's located in was built in 1864 and is now fully restored. It's located at the corner of King and Picton Sts.

Other places to keep an eye out for in Niagara-On-the-Lake are **McLelland's Store, The Fudge Shop,** and **Greaves Jam.** Just south of town near St. David's is the **Orchard Glen Market.** The market is a good place to buy fruit, especially strawberries, cherries, peaches, and apples. It's open from June through October. There's a craft store that you might want to visit in Niagara-On-the-Lake called **The Gingham Patch.** It features gifts, toys, Mennonite quilts, and Quebec weaving. The store is located at 75 Queen St.

Nipigon

The **Nipigon Museum and Gallery** is a good place to familiarize yourself with some of the north's most prominent characteristics. It includes displays relating to native culture, the logging industry, the fur trade, and rocks and minerals of the region. Another feature of this museum is the **L.M. Lein Gallery of Archeology.** The museum is open daily from mid-June to early September.

Norwich

The **Norwich and District Museum** features items relating to the history and culture of the Quakers in the area. In fact the museum itself is situated in a former meeting house of the Society of Friends. The museum also has displays depicting the early life of the pioneers, including household articles, crafts, Indian artifacts, a general store, and a children's corner. It's open in the afternoons from May until Thanksgiving on Wednesdays, weekends, and public holidays.

Oakville

If you'd like to do some shopping with a little more interest and fun than supermarkets and department stores, come to Oakville. You can harvest your own pears, beans, tomatoes, and other vegetables at **U-Pick Farms** just north of the Third Line via the North Service Road. They're open from late June until late October.

If you're in Oakville on a Sunday, there's a chance you can pick up some good stuff at the **Granary Antique Market.** It's open in the afternoons of the first and third Sunday of each month.

While you're in the area, you might enjoy a trip to Bronte,

southwest of Oakville. **Bronte Provincial Park** features a working, turn of the century farm as well as a separate children's farm with animals the kids can pet and a barn with lots of hay to jump in, ropes to swing on, and barrels to roll. The park also offers tractor and wagon tours. It's open year round with limited facilities in the winter.

There's a craft store in Bronte that might also be worth visiting. **The Old Bronte Post Office Gallery** at 86 Bronte Road contains crafts by many local artists. It features pottery, weaving, jewellery, quilts, wooden toys, and many other items.

The store is closed on Mondays and Tuesdays. Another local craft store is **Gifted Hands.** It carries work by a number of Ontario craftspeople. Their crafts include jewellery, pottery, leaded glass, and weaving.

There's an old fashioned country patisserie and tea room in Oakville that bills itself as the nation's oldest. **The Continental Pastry Shop** at 170 Lakeshore Rd. E., serves lunches and afternoon tea daily.

Oil Springs

With Canada's oil reserves becoming so important in recent years, interest in the **Oil Museum of Canada** should be high. The museum is located off Highway 21 and is open from late May until late October, as well as on weekends during November. This museum traces the discovery of the first commercialized oil well in North America. Early drilling equipment is on display, and drill rigs have been set up on the grounds.

Orillia

Orillia is best known as the home of Canadian humourist Stephen Leacock and as the thinly veiled scenario of his *Sunshine Sketches of a Little Town.* So a visit to Orillia would not be complete without seeing the **Stephen Leacock Memorial House.** The house is situated near Old Brewery Bay and contains exhibits of Leacock's private papers, letters, and personal notes. It also features the original hand-written manuscript for *Sunshine Sketches* which was purchased in 1966 for $21,000.

You can have a look at some old railway memorabilia and enjoy a good meal at the same time with a visit to the **Ossawippi Express** restaurant at 210 Mississauga St. W. The restaurant features an array of turn-of-the-century railway cars, and you can dine in original mahogany-panelled interiors amidst railway artifacts.

Something that children will be sure to enjoy is a trip to the **L.B.K. Ranch,** 12 km north of Highway 11 on the eighth concession of Oro. You take a special bus over trails in the bush to see moose, buffalo, elk, deer, and other animals. It's open daily from July to Labour Day and on weekends only the rest of the time between Victoria Day and October.

Daylight saving time

There are many occupations traditionally associated with cunning and deceptive business practices. But the last one you'd suspect would be the farmer. So now, who can you trust?

Poultry farmers have been known to dupe poor, helpless chicks into laying more eggs. In fall and winter they sometimes use artificial lights with an automatic timer to lengthen the hours of daylight in the mind of the chick and increase egg production. They employ the same trick for a different reason with ducklings. When they want to fatten them up, they use lights at night to increase feed consumption. The question is: Why won't ducklings eat in the dark? Are they simply too afraid to eat or are they like cynical restaurant patrons who suspect that dim, romantic lighting is merely a scheme to disguise substandard food.

Northwest of Orillia near Coldwater, you can dine at **The Farm House,** a turn-of-the-century style restaurant on Mt. St. Louis Rd. Southwest of Orillia, there's an interesting shop in Craighurst. **Craighurst Innantiques** specializes in antique jewellery, country furniture, and Canadian folk and native art.

Oshawa

Trace the Canadian auto industry from its beginnings in 1898 to the present in the **Canadian Automobile Museum**. The museum houses about 50 vintage cars as well as models and photographic displays. It's located at 99 Simcoe St. S. and is open daily, year round.

The Family Tree at 10 King St. is a good place to shop for pottery, weaving, glassware, leatherwork, toys, and paintings. East of Oshawa at Kendal there's another good place to shop for crafts. **Kendal Hill Arts, Crafts, and Antiques** is located on RR1 at the foot of the Oshawa Ski Club hill. This store carries work by a number of local crafstpeople. The crafts include weaving, leather, pottery, and braided rugs. It's open from mid-May to mid-October in the afternoons from Wednesday to Sunday, as well as holiday Mondays.

There's a good fruit market that's also east of Oshawa. **Fred's Fruit Market** in Orono specializes in pick-your-own strawberries. It also sells apples, pears, cider, and sweet corn over the counter. It's open daily, year-round and is situated at Highways 115 and 35, just south of Orono.

Just west of Oshawa at the Pickering Sheraton Mall at Liverpool Rd. and Highway 401 is the **East Metro Flea Market.** It's open every Sunday, year round.

Ottawa

Not many cities can claim to have a farm operating within their boundaries but that's exactly the case in Ottawa. The **Central Experimental Farm** is comprised of 1200 acres of land and features crops, livestock, greenhouses, an arboretum, and flower gardens.

There's also a large farmer's market in Ottawa. The **Byward Market** attracts farmers from the Ottawa Valley as well as some from Quebec. There are parks and museums in Ottawa to suit almost any interest or type of recreation. There are also a number of good ski areas within easy driving distance of the city.

Just west of town on Highway 7 at Stittsville is **Gibson's Antique and Flea Market.** It's open on Sundays.

Owen Sound

You can view many of the works and possessions of one of Canada's most famous painters at the **Tom Thomson Memorial Art Gallery** in Owen Sound. There are also a number of other paintings of nineteenth and twentieth century Canadian artists on display there. It's situated at 840 1st Avenue West.

Another place to visit in Owen Sound is **The County of Grey and Owen Sound Museum.** This museum traces the geological and natural history of Grey county. Its displays include early pioneer household articles, gadgets and tools, clothing, furniture, and even log houses. There are occasional displays of wool spinning, harness making, blacksmithing, and quilting. The museum is open daily during July and August and afternoons only, except Mondays, for the rest of the year.

If you're shopping in Owen Sound you might enjoy browsing at **Carol's Antiques and Collectibles** at 299 Tenth St. E. This store specializes in Canadian and British interior furnishings. There's also a **Farmer's Market** in Owen Sound. It's open on Saturdays and has some craft items as well as produce. If you're travelling south from the city, there's an antique dealer in Chatsworth you could visit. **Junction Antiques** is found at the intersection of Highways 6 and 10.

Grow your own

Many of the wild flowers and plants found in forests and fields can be successfully transplanted and grown at home. Perhaps the most interesting to attempt is Ontario's floral emblem, the white Trillium.

You can buy white trillium plants at some nurseries, or you can bring your own back from the woods. You'll need to take a shovel, plastic bags, and don't forget the insect repellent.

Trilliums can be transplanted at any time of year, but the best time seems to be the fall, when the plant is fairly dormant. Try not to disturb the roots; it's a good idea to keep a clump of soil around them. When you get them home plant them in a spot with good drainage, out of direct summer sun. Heavy clay or sandy soils do not support the plant well.

A little loving care will result in beautiful blooms each spring. Do not attempt to bring the bloom indoors: although picking does not kill the plant, it does weaken the roots and the plant will not bloom again for seven or eight years.

Pakenham

If you're in the area of Pakenham and you're looking for a good selection of crafts, you can visit **Andrew Dickson's Large and Splendid Two-Storey Dwelling.** Not only is it large and splendid, but it's old too. The house was built in 1840 and now features the work of many local craftspeople. It features a wide variety of crafts including ceramics, weaving, clothing, puppets, and many other fine goods.

Pembroke

There are a couple of good museums to visit in Pembroke. **The Champlain Trail Museum** at 1032 Pembroke St. has exhibits relating to the fur trade, the story of pioneer settlers in the area, and the beginnings of the lumber industry. One of the highlights of the museum is an exact replica of an astrolabe that Champlain lost in the area. The museum also includes a log cabin, a smokehouse, an outdoor bake oven, a carriage shed, a workshop, and a farm implement shed. There are also examples of old fashioned farm machinery on the grounds. The museum is open from June to Labour Day.

Another museum of note in the city is the **Algonquin Indian History Museum.** It contains a variety of Indian artifacts and features some birch bark canoes. It's situated on an Indian reserve, just south of Highway 60 at Golden Lake and is open on Mondays, Wednesdays, and weekends from Victoria Day to Labour Day.

For the adventurous, there are one and two day **Whitewater Canoe Trips** through the rapids of the Ottawa and Petawawa Rivers, conducted by expert guides. All equipment is provided as well as return shuttle service to Pembroke. These trips are for good swimmers only, participants must be at least 15 years old, and advance reservations are required. Write Wilderness Tours, Box 661, Pembroke.

Just 7 km east of Pembroke you can see a wide variety of native and exotic animals at the **Stone Hill Animal Farm.** You can reach this working farm by travelling on Highway 17 to County Road 21, turning right after 3 km and following the signs.

Penetanguishene

History buffs will enjoy visiting the **Historic Naval and Military Establishments** in Penetanguishene. These buildings are authentic recreations of military and pioneer settlements in the early days of the British Empire. Tour guides will take you through restored workshops, a naval storehouse, officer's quarters, offices, residences, and gunpoints. Regimental soldiers also give demonstrations of parade drills and musketry.

You might also enjoy taking one of the boat cruises offered through the islands of Georgian Bay. You can get aboard the **Georgian Queen** at the town dock any day from June to September. Before you board the ship why not take a look at some of the crafts offered at **The Sea Gull** at the town dock. This craft store carries the work of local artists and includes a wide variety of crafts.

Petawawa

You can learn about forest ecology at the **Petawawa Forest Experimental Station.** The station covers 38 square miles of forest. Walking tours are guided by the staff of the station who explain the kind of research being carried out there. It is located on Highway 17 and is open daily from June to mid-September.

Trees are not the only thing grown in the Petawawa region. You can prove this to yourself by visiting **Gourmet Farms Ltd.** and sampling some of their fresh produce. They even have greenhouse crops outside the normal vegetable seasons. Their specialties include potatoes, corn, tomatoes, maple syrup, and honey. They're open daily, year round.

Playing it cool

If you've tried fishing in the summer and found it too hot, too complicated, and too expensive, then ice fishing may be more to your liking. You won't have the bother of hot weather, insects, boats, or complicated casting mechanisms. And your equipment should be cheaper and simpler to use.

Safety is the first concern on an ice fishing trip and one must always be aware of the possibility of ice giving out. One good way to be sure a body of water is safe to fish is to look for one that already has ice fishermen on it. You could also ask officials at a district office of the Ministry of Natural Resources.

All you need to go ice fishing is an ice breaking tool, an ice scoop, an ice fishing rod or tip-up, lures, and/or bait. The ice breaking tool is used to make the hole you'll fish through and there are several different kinds available. There's an ordinary axe, a drill-like instrument called an ice auger, or a long, sharp, spade-like tool called a spud.

There is at least one advantage of the spud from a safety point of view. If you carry a spud horizontally as you walk across the ice, it may enable you to pull yourself up out of the water should you fall through.

Once you've made a hole in the ice and started fishing, you should periodically clear the hole of thin pieces of ice that start to form. This is where the scoop comes in handy.

Rods used for ice fishing are very simple. They're much shorter than ordinary rods and don't have reels. Since lines tend to freeze up, strikes are reeled in by hand. You simply hold the rod over the hole and jig it up and down for the best results. If you're using live bait, jigging is not so crucial since fish will be attracted by the movement of the bait. Fish often head for the shelter of weeds right at the bottom of a lake during winter. So it's a good idea to check the depth with a weight on the end of your line and begin fishing about a foot from the bottom. Once you've tried awhile at that depth, experiment if you don't get good results.

The alternative to a rod is a tip-up. A tip-up is a rod that stands upright in the hole; you don't have to hold it. A cross piece keeps it from sinking through the hole, and the line is completely submerged so it doesn't freeze up. You must watch the tip-up because when a strike is made, a spring releases and a small flag goes up, and you must go and land the fish. Sometimes floating bobbers are used instead of flags, in which case you watch for the bobber to submerge when a strike occurs.

Regardless of whether you use bobbers or flags, you can sit back and relax or hop around to keep warm while keeping an eye on them. As you also might have guessed, fishing with tip-ups enables you to have several lines in the water at once,

continued on next page

however there are regulations concerning this and you should contact the Ministry of Natural Resources to check them out. There are also regulations concerning attending to the tip-ups.

If you don't get strikes right away, be patient and optimistic. While noises above the ice like conversation won't scare fish away, noise made while digging the hole in the ice might. So you might have to wait a short while before they return.

Lakes that are good for fishing in summer generally provide good ice fishing too. However, the best way to find a good spot is to talk to local fishermen. And they should be co-operative since there are enough fish to go around. Many people say that you can get as many or more fish than in summer, especially if you're using more than one tip-up.

Ice fishing also has an advantage for the squeamish. If you've always felt uncomfortable about taking a squirming fish off a hook, you can sidestep the problem when ice fishing. Just leave the fish on the hook until it's frozen solid and take out the hook at home when it's dead and thawed out.

Wearing warm and waterproof clothing is essential to an ice fisherman. But if the cold does slow you down a little, it may encourage you to know that it slows down the fish too. Experts say that fish are known not to put up as good a fight when hooked in the winter.

Peterborough

If you're heading for the Kawartha Lakes region of Ontario, chances are you'll pass by Peterborough. And there are many good reasons to stop. During July and August you can take advantage of the excellent repertory theatre productions of **Peterborough Summer Theatre.** Plays are held in the air conditioned comfort of the Wenjack Theatre at Trent University.

Any set of locks in operation seems to attract a great deal of interest, so the **Hydraulic Lift Lock** in Peterborough should keep you fascinated. It literally lifts the boats and the water they're in, 20 metres in the air! The locks are in operation from June to September and are busiest on the weekends. If that doesn't satisfy your nautical inquisitiveness you can see a working model of the Trent-Severn Waterway at the **Peterborough Centennial Museum.** The museum also includes minerals and fossils, Indian and pioneer artifacts, paintings, and sculpture. It's situated on Hunter St. E. and is open daily, year round.

Another place to visit in this city is practical, but fun. The **Farmer's Market** in Peterborough is open every Saturday morning at Morrow Park.

If you're interested in antiques, Peterborough has **Crown Antiques** at 283 George St. N. It's open during the day from Tuesday to Saturday as well as other times by appointment.

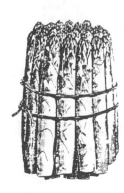

Picton

Enjoy the relaxed, small town atmosphere of Picton. A good place to dine in Picton is the **Inn on the Bay,** at 73 Bridge St. This home was built in the early 1800s and is furnished with antique pieces. There is a patio for outdoor dining in the summer.

You can get out in the sunshine and pick your own strawberries and vegetables at **Leavitt Bros. Farm** on County Road 1, just 8 km west of town. It's open daily from mid-June to the end of October.

If you're travelling south of Picton you might want to stop at **Nurcombe's Weaving Studio** in Cherry Valley. You can view demonstrations of hand weaving and spinning there daily.

Port Colborne

You'll find some interesting antique glassware at the **Port Colborne Historical and Marine Museum.** Some of this glassware was produced at the Erie Glass Company which operated in the town from 1892-1894. The museum also has displays of articles pertaining to the early history of the area, and in particular, the Welland Canal. It's open daily during the afternoons in July and August and on weekday afternoons during May, June, September, October, and November.

If you work up an appetite in Port Colborne, it shouldn't present a problem. One premiere dining spot is the **Rathfon Inn** on Lakeshore Rd., just west of town. The Inn was built in 1800 as a family home. The building has real old-world character as it is surrounded by a 4 foot high limestone wall.

If you're on the run and you want to pick up some fruit or vegetables you can visit the **Farmer's Market.** It's situated in the Market Square of Port Colborne and features home cooked goods as well as the standard fruit and vegetable fare.

Port Hope

This pretty lakeside town is an ideal place to enjoy some fine country hospitality. **Penryn Park** at 82 Victoria St. S. is a family estate built in 1859. The house features many beautiful pieces of furniture owned by the original family living there. The restaurant serves up continental cuisine and specializes in homemade desserts and fresh baked pastries. Another place to relax and enjoy good food is the **Pine Ridge Lodge** in Bewdley, just north of Port Hope on Highway 28. This restaurant offers an excellent view and fine French-Canadian food.

Up with insects

The next time you find yourself cursing the mosquitos at the cottage or the ants at your picnic, try to remember that we need insects.

Insects pollinate many plants that would otherwise be unable to reproduce. They also contribute to the growth of plants since their burrowing in the soil tills the earth and adds nutrients to it. Without insects, many plant species would diminish in number or simply die out.

The absence of insects in our environment would have quite a "domino effect." Not only do some animals feed on the plants that insects aid, but the insects themselves provide food for birds. And the effect that diminishing numbers of birds and animals would have on our ecology would be vast.

However, despite the various ecological benefits of insects, it's hard to see past the red spots on your arms or listen to reason while they're buzzing in your ears. So here are a few tips to keep them at bay.

Insects are attracted more to certain colours, particularly red, dark blue, and dark green. Certain odours will also bring them flying or crawling in your direction. Besides food, anything sweet smelling attracts them, such as cologne, perfume, or even freshly washed hair. One suggestion for keeping them away at night is to burn orange and lemon peels in your campfire. But keep in mind that a diet of oranges and lemons each evening may keep you running all night.

Richmond Hill (and nearby towns)

Richmond Hill, and the towns around it are proof that you can enjoy some fun country times without going too far from Toronto. At the Lion's Hall at 106 Centre St. E. in Richmond Hill, there's an **Antique Show and Sale** held on the first Sunday of each month. There's a similar event happening on the third Sunday of each month between September and June in Woodbridge, just southwest of Richmond Hill. The **Antique Market and Show** is held at the Woodbridge Arena at Islington Avenue and Highway 7. If Saturdays are a better day for you to browse through the small towns around Toronto, you can visit the **Stouffville Sale Barn.** Activities held there include an antique market, a flea market, a produce market, and a bake sale. The barn is open year round and it's located off Highway 48.

King City, northwest of Richmond Hill is a good place to harvest your own produce. **Pine Farms Orchard** is open for picking your own apples by reservation on weekdays and all day on the weekends. It's situated just 2 km west of town, 4 km north on Jane St. and then east 1 km on Green Line. **Farmer Jack's Gardens** has facilities for picking your own tomatoes, peppers and sweet corn. There is also a market where you can get home baked pies. The farm is open daily and is situated on Kennedy Rd., 8 km north of Highway 7. Another market is located 10 km north of Highway 7 on the Gormley-Stouffville Rd. between Highway 48 and Woodbine Avenue.

Ridgetown

One of the best things to do in Ridgetown is to visit the **Ridge House Museum Gallery.** The house was built in 1875 and has been restored with furnishings from that time. The gallery includes pioneer household goods, furniture, various artifacts, and folk art. It's open from April to December on Wednesday, Saturday, and Sunday afternoons.

If you're in Ridgetown on a Saturday in the summer, you might want to visit the **Youth and Family Market** held every Saturday morning from July to September at the East Kent Arena.

If you're travelling southwest past Blenheim, be sure to keep an eye open for **Eastman's Fruit Market** on Highway 3. This market specializes in peaches, apples, and wine grapes.

Rockton

You'll know when you're approaching this town by the roar of the lions from the **African Lion Safari** situated there. A drive through this park in the safety of your own car or a bus that is provided takes you close to roaming animals such as tigers, hyenas, elephants, ostriches, camels, antelopes, rare white rhinos, and monkeys. The park features over 1,000 exotic animals and birds. The park also has an African Curio Shop, a cafeteria, and an outdoor cafe. It's open daily from March to November, and on weekends only the rest of the year.

A less exotic, but nonetheless interesting place to visit in the Rockton area is the **Wentworth**

Pioneer Village, off Highway 52. The Village consists of 27 reconstructed buildings that recreate the spirit of pioneer days. These buildings include an old fashioned drug store, a railway station, an Indian log church, and a general store. There are also nature trails and picnic facilities on the premises.

Rockwood

Just outside Rockwood you'll find the **Streetcar and Electric Railway Museum.** Here you can see a variety of historic streetcars, most of them at least 50 years old. Listen to the sounds of a bygone era as you ride an old fashioned train on a scenic mile of track through rural Ontario. Enjoy the clang of the bell, the throb of the air compressor, and the sound of the whistle! The museum is open Saturday, Sunday, and holidays in the afternoons, from Victoria Day to the last week in October.

St. Catharines

St. Catharines is located in the rich agricultural region of the Niagara Peninsula. And many of the attractions of the town are related to food and agriculture. One highlight of a trip to St. Catharines would be taking the **Jordan Wine Tour.** This is a tour of the winery that includes tasting opportunities. The winery is located at 120 Ridley Road and is open Monday to Friday, year round.

Another interesting place to visit in this city is **Stokes Seeds.** Gardens across the country owe their existence to this place. Anyone with a green thumb or aspirations to one will enjoy viewing the mass plantings of a wide variety of different species and colours. They're open on weekdays from

June to September at their location on Martindale Rd.

If you want to buy some fresh produce you can get it from the farmers without leaving the city at the **St. Catharines Farmer's Market.** Being part of the Niagara Fruit Belt, the market is well known for its fruit as well as vegetables. It's located between City Hall and the Federal Building and is open year round on Tuesdays, Thursdays, and Saturdays. With all the food that is produced in the area, it helps to have something nice to eat off. Why not pick up a fine china plate at the **Town House,** 216 King St. Antique dishes are just one of its specialties.

St. Jacob's

The tiny village of St. Jacob's features a beautiful main street lined with interesting shops that reflect the Pennsylvania Dutch heritage of the region. Wood decor in the solid, clean lines of the Mennonite tradition, and locally fired brick exteriors create a warm, charming atmosphere for leisurely browsing. Some of the shops and their specialties include: **Century House Antiques** — antiques and local crafts; **Canadian Traditions** — handcrafted pine reproduction furniture; **The Schnitzelbank** — crafts and wickerware; **The Stone Crock Restaurant** — Pennsylvania Dutch cuisine; **Women's Weaving and Variety** — durable, hand-woven scatter mats and made to order hall and stair runners; and the **Laughing Horse Gallery** — photography. There's a **Gift Shop** and **The Village Bakery** attached to the Stone Crock Restaurant as well. You can also watch a skilled craftsman pursuing an old trade at **Jan B. Martin's Blacksmith Shop.**

Barnstorming

When driving along on country roads in Ontario, why not take a closer look at some of the barns you see. Watch for paintings on the sides which often depict farm animals or landscapes. In areas of Pennsylvania-Dutch heritage in southern Ontario, you may notice hex symbols painted on barns. They are colourful geometric symbols, originally painted to protect the cattle within from witches.

Paintings are not the only thing to look for. Many barns have weather vanes attached to small spires which feature farm animals. The rooster is the most common ornament, however you just might spot the occasional fish or horse.

Another common element on barns is the lightning rod. Watch for rods with glass balls attached to them. They are decorative, but when broken, they tell the farmer that it's been struck.

St. Mary's

There are some impressive, old stone buildings in St. Mary's. One of them is the **St. Mary's District Museum.** This museum has displays relating to the pioneers and early settlements in the area. It is located at 177 Church St. S. and is open from May through October from Tuesday to Saturday in the afternoons. The **Westover Park Guest House** is a stone building where you can get a good meal.

If you're interested in antiques you might check out **Ruth Irvine Antiques** at 32 St. Andrew's St. This shop specializes in glassware, china, and jewellery. Another antique dealer in town is **Stonetown Antiques** at 14 Church St. N. It specializes in Canadiana, especially furniture, prints, and books. **The Collector's Shop** in nearby Kirkton is another worthwhile stop for antique hunters. It carries antiques, collectibles, furniture, stoves, bottles, and fruit jars. The store is open every afternoon during July and August, but only on weekend afternoons during the rest of the year.

St. Thomas

There's lots of greenery in St. Thomas. **Waterworks Park** features a fine floral display and is an excellent spot for a family picnic. **Pinafore Park** includes a wildlife sanctuary and offers rides on a unique, narrow-gauge, steam engine railway. There's even some green available in the winter at **Swain Greenhouses.** Explore three acres of house plants, cacti, and succulents in a tropical atmosphere and buy if you so desire.

If you're looking for fresh produce you can visit **Wood Lynn Farms Ltd.** at 184 Sunset Drive. It specializes in pick-your-own cherries and apples in season, plus fresh meat and produce. There's a similar kind of operation just north of St. Thomas in the Talbotville area. **Talbotville Fruit Market** is located 1 km north of town. It features pick-your-own strawberries, raspberries, and vegetables. It's open from mid-May to mid-November.

Sarnia

There's a unique museum located on Highway 40, just five miles south of town. **The Pilot House Museum** is a Great Lakes Oil tanker's centre castle. It is restored to its original condition and serves to illustrate what life on the ships is like. It includes the wheel house, compass engine room telegraph, chart table, signal flag locker, officer's quarters, and masters' quarters. The museum is open from May to mid-October all day from Monday to Saturday and in the afternoons on Sundays.

The Upstairs Gallery in Sarnia features pottery and weaving. It's situated at 300 N. Christian St. and is open from Tuesday to Saturday. **The Candle Factory** at 1392 London features handmade candles. If antiques are your area of interest, there's **House of Hartwell Fine Antiques** at 290 N. Christian St. You'll find more antiques in nearby Petrolia at **Quality Antiques** at 419 King St.

There's a park that children would probably enjoy to the northwest of Sarnia at Point Edward. **Canatara Park** includes a children's farm complete with friendly livestock and poultry. There are also facilities for swimming and picnics.

Sault Ste. Marie

This city, located on the east side of Lake Superior, is a marine centre. So a good place to start when visiting is the **Marine Museum** at 41 Lake St. This museum features many authentic marine records and artifacts. Many of the items on display have been recovered through underwater archeology. The museum is open daily from early June until Labour Day. Another attraction in Sault Ste. Marie is the museum ship **Norgoma**, the last overnight passenger cruise ship ever built on the Great Lakes.

You can also watch the sea-going ships of many nations and long lake freighters pass through the Soo Locks, which connect Lake Huron and Lake Superior. The best view of the ships and the locks is afforded by the ship that will take you on a **Lock Tour**. These tours are offered daily from June until early October.

One of the most interesting things on the mainland in Sault Ste. Marie is the **Ermatinger Old Stone House.** Built in 1814, it is said to be the oldest stone house in Canada, west of Toronto. It was built by Charles Oakes Ermatinger, a fur trader. Part of the house includes displays describing the Ermatinger family, the fur trade, and other events of local historical interest. The house is also furnished in the early nineteenth century period in which it was built. It's located at 831 Queen St. and is open from April through November on weekdays, and daily from June to the end of September.

There are some good road and rail tours offered in the area. **The Algoma Central Railway** takes you to the Agawa Canyon, an unspoiled area of waterfalls, mountains, ravines, and forests that is only accessible by rail. In summer, the tours are available from June until mid-October, but there are also opportunities to ride the snow train on weekends from January through March. You can also explore Sault Ste. Marie and surrounding area on a **Hiawathaland Sightseeing Tour.** These bus tours are available from mid-June to Labour Day weekend.

There's a craft store in town that you might also like to visit. **The Loon's Nest** at Bay and Bruce Sts. features quilts, weaving, pottery, puppets, dolls, paintings, and Inuit and Indian crafts. Southeast of Sault Ste. Marie near Thessalon is a craft outlet called **The Round Barn.** It is in fact located in a round barn on a farm on RR2 (Brownlee Rd). It sells Canadian handicrafts, kitchen specialty items, and oil paintings. It's open from Victoria Day until Thanksgiving.

Snowball

There are some great, country style places to shop in Snowball and nearby Kettleby. If you're looking for some good food, your first stop should be **The Country Gourmet.** This store has a good selection of gourmet food, teas, cheese, custom blended coffee, and gift items.

Children will enjoy the selection of unusual toys found at **Mostly Dolls.** It features many different kinds of dolls as well as stuffed animals.

Just northwest of Snowball in Kettleby is another old fashioned store you'll want to visit. The **Kettleby Country Store** offers quality pine and walnut furniture and china in a country setting. It's open from Wednesday to Sunday. Another place where you could look for some fine country furniture is **Landmark House.** This store features pine antiques. It's located in Kettleby Village and it's open Saturday, Sunday, and Monday afternoons.

Another store to visit in the area is the **Kettleby Village General Store.** Two of its claims to fame are their hand-dipped ice cream cones and their pine and gift shop.

Stoney Creek

This town is located within the boundaries of the Niagara Fruit Belt and that explains the two pick-your-own fruit farms in the area. The **Punch Bowl Fruit Boutique** specializes in cherries, plums, pears, and grapes that you can harvest yourself in season. You can also get dried fruit and nuts there. To get there, take Highway 20 south 2 km from town to Ridge Road, turn east and go 2 km. It's open from May through October. The **Tigchelaar Berry Farm** features pick-your-own strawberries and raspberries. To get there, take Highway 56 south to Golf Club Road, turn east and continue to Hendershot Road, then turn south. It's open from mid-June to mid-August.

One of the older military buildings in Ontario is found in Stoney Creek. The **Historic Battlefield Museum** was built in 1795 and it is now fully restored to depict military life in the early 1800s. It is also the site of a monument built in 1913 to commemorate fallen British and American soldiers killed in the Battle of June 6th, 1813.

Stratford

One of the most popular things to do in Ontario during the summer is to visit the **Stratford Shakespearean Festival.** It features world renowned actors and actresses in some of Shakespeare's greatest works as well as contemporary plays. There are also several nights of music at Stratford featuring opera or folk singers. The Festival runs from June to mid-October.

There are several fine country dining spots in the Stratford area. **Fryfogel's Inn and Museum** was built in 1844 and has now been restored and furnished to that time period. Another fine old building where you can get a good meal in Stratford is the **Church Restaurant.** Enjoy their French cuisine and admire this century old church's Gothic arches, carved woodwork, and stained glass windows. It's situated at 70 Brunswick St.

There's a craft store you might enjoy in Stratford called **The Carriage House.** It's located in a 110 year old building at 330 Ontario St. and it includes pottery, weaving, stained glass, and jewellery.

Cheese connoisseurs will be interested in a visit to **Tavistock Union Cheese and Butter Ltd.** Tavistock is just a few miles southeast of Stratford so it's well worth the trip. This company has been manufacturing cheese since 1879. The cheese shop there is open Monday to Friday.

Strathroy

The Strathroy Middlesex Museum is unique in that it houses displays that celebrate the past and the present. The home it is located in was built in 1871 and it contains many exhibits relating to the early settlers of the area. These include a miniature doll house in the Victorian style and a restored old time print shop. On the other side of the coin are displays relating to art, communications, industry, recreation, and science. One of the highlights of this aspect of the museum is the computer room. The museum is located at 84 Oxford St., and is open in the afternoons every day but Saturday, from May to December. From February to April, it's open Wednesday, Friday, and Sunday afternoons.

Just two miles south of Strathroy there's an **Old Country Store** that you might enjoy. It's situated on Highway 81 and specializes in Inuit art, Indian handmade moccasins, and other examples of Canadiana.

Sudbury

Sudbury is probably the largest mining city in Ontario and its residents are proud of it. Evidence of this can be found in **Canadian Centennial Numismatic Park** where there stands a 30 foot high stainless steel Canadian nickel as well as other giant coins. The park also has a replica of a working mine to explore as well as a model steam train which circles it. It's open from late May to Thanksgiving. If a replica of a mine doesn't suit you, how about a tour of the real thing? **Mine Tours** of Inco are offered daily except Sundays from mid-May to Labour Day. Falconbridge has tours from mid-June to mid-September except during July and on Sundays.

A tour of the mines will assure you that there are many hard-working pairs of hands in Sudbury, but a trip to 137 Durham St. S. will convince you that there are also **Creative Hands.** This is a craft store which features work in ceramics, leather, jewellery, batik, and weaving.

Terra Cotta

If you're interested in crafts, antiques, or good restaurants you'll enjoy Terra Cotta and surrounding areas. The **Terra Cotta Inn** is a country dining spot located in a frame house built in the nineteenth century on 50 acres of land by the Credit River. Tea is served on the patio in the summer. The Inn is open daily except Mondays in the summer months, and Friday, Saturday, and Sunday evenings for dinner during the winter. Sunday brunch is available year round.

The Forge is a craft store worth visiting that specializes in pottery, glass, embroidery, weaving, and jewellery among other things. It's situated on RR1 and is open afternoons from Tuesday to Sunday from May to December. Just northwest of Terra Cotta in Inglewood on Highway 10 is **John's Antiques.** They buy and sell good, old furniture.

Thornbury

Thornbury and nearby towns have many of the good things the country has to offer. One of those good things is a farm outlet called **Goldsmith Orchards.** It's specialties are apples, fresh cider, sweet corn, and potatoes. The Orchards are located just west of town on Highway 26 and are open from early August until late December.

Something else that often crops up in the country is an antique store. **J's Antiques** is situated one and a half blocks south of the lights at Thornbury and it specializes in china, glass, and furniture.

Northwest of Thornbury at Meaford is a craft store called **Muffin 'N Mouse.** Its wares include Canadiana, art, ceramics, quilts, and dolls. The store is situated across from the museum in town.

On the other side of Thornbury via Highway 26 is Craigleith and the **Craigleith Depot Restaurant.** This restaurant is located in an old railway station which includes a variety of gay nineties memorabilia.

Thunder Bay

A merger of the twin cities of Fort William and Port Arthur, the city of Thunder Bay is "the gateway to the west." The nineteen huge grain elevators situated there are proof that this is not just a cliche. One of the elevators, Saskatchewan Pool 7, is the largest single-unit working elevator in the world. Enough grain is stored in this elevator to make two loaves of bread for every person in North America! Tourists can visit these elevators in the summer so if you're interested, check with the Visitors Information Bureau at 193 Arthur St. While these grain elevators may contain a piece of the west, you can find a piece of the south at the city's **Botanical Gardens.** They feature plants ranging from banana plants and palm trees to hibiscus blossoms.

One of the big historical attractions in Ontario can be found in Thunder Bay. **Old Fort William** is a reconstruction of the inland headquarters of the North West Company. The Fort was a major fur trading centre for the northern explorers and the Voyageurs from Quebec. The staff at the Fort attempts to recreate some of the activities that went on there some 150 years ago. Visitors can help them build huge birch bark canoes, test fire a musket, watch the activity in the pack stores, enjoy some oven baked fresh bread, or enjoy a hearty bowl of stew. Other areas of historical interest in Thunder Bay are the **Logging Museum** in Centennial Park during the summers, and the **Thunder Bay Museum** at 219 May St. S. The **National Exhibition Centre** also includes displays of history as well as some relating to art and culture.

There's also an **Amethyst Mine** in the area where visitors can go searching for the beautiful purple stone. It's open from May to November, weather permitting.

One of the most renowned craftspeople in Ontario operates out of Thunder Bay. Dena Mayhew Dahl makes puppets which are sold across Canada. You can find her store, **Dahl House Designs Ltd.** at 341 Empress Avenue. Another craft store in town specializes in stained glass and supplies for making it. The store is the **Glass Menagerie** and it's located at 38 Court St. S. There's also a wide variety of crafts available at **Handmade House** at 420 Victoria Avenue. Thunder Bay is also a great area for skiers. At last count there are five ski areas operating in the vicinity as well as the **Big Thunder Ski Jump.** Even if you aren't the one tackling the 90 and 70 metre jumps, it's a thrilling sport to watch.

Trenton

The Trenton area is good for browsers. You might start with a visit to the **Quinte Flea Market** on Saturdays and Sundays. It's situated at Highway 401 and Glen Miller Road. Another interesting place to poke around is **Irene's Antiques** on Highway 33, south of town. The store specializes in pine, English furniture, fine art glass, collectibles, and unusual items. North of Trenton on Highway 33 is the town of Stirling where you'll find a **Flea Market** every Sunday from May to October. It's held at the Stirling fairgrounds.

There's no guarantee you'll find an antique item to suit you in Trenton, but it is likely that you'll get exactly what you want at **Bonter's Bayview Orchards,** west of Belleville. If you poke around the fields at the right time of year you're sure to come up with some strawberries, apples, or tomatoes. This pick-your-own operation is complemented by a market which sells sweet corn. This market is open on weekends the year round and daily from July to mid-October. It's located on Rednesville Rd. (County Rd. 3).

Vineland

Examine some of the great tourist sites in the world, scaled down to one fiftieth of their actual size at **Tivoli-On-the-Lake.** The model buildings include the Eiffel Tower, St. Peter's Basilica, the Tower of Pisa, Cologne Cathedral, and the Kremlin. It's accessible by either the Prudhomme Blvd. or Victoria Avenue exit of the Q.E.W., and is open daily from mid-April to Thanksgiving.

While you're in the Vineland area, you might want to take advantage of some of the fresh fruit outlets. **Cherry Avenue Farms Ltd.** specializes in pick-your-own cherries, peaches, apricots, plums, pears, and grapes. You can get there by taking the Vineland exit off the Q.E.W., turning right on Victoria Avenue South and watching for signs. It's open from mid-June until mid-October.

An interesting craft store in Vineland is **Rittermere Crafts** on Cherry Avenue. This store specializes in hooked rugs. It's open year-round except for July.

Wasaga Beach

This town is located on the southern shores of Georgian Bay. While you're near the water, it's worth a trip out to Nancy Island and the **Museum of the Upper Lakes** located there. The museum includes naval artifacts, models, photographs, and displays which trace the 300 year history of shipping on the upper lakes. The remains of the schooner Nancy that was destroyed in the War of 1812 are on the grounds of the main building. An electronic theatre show portrays the destruction of the Nancy and the subsequent capture of the ships that attacked her. The Museum is open daily from Victoria Day to Labour Day and on weekend afternoons from Labour Day to Thanksgiving.

Another attraction of Wasaga Beach is the **Wildlife Park** there. The park contains over 800 animals and birds in a mainly natural bush setting. The animals found there include elephants, hippos, jaguars, wallabies, emus, and vultures. It's located on Zoo Park Rd. and is open from late May until Thanksgiving.

There are several places to buy crafts in the Wasaga Beach area. **Osborne's Castle Gifts** carries wicker items, pottery, parkas, homemade jams and jellies, and other craft items. It's situated 2km east of the bridge on Highway 92. South of Wasaga Beach on RR3 at Stayner is a store called **Huronia Handcrafted Gifts.** It specializes in Hudson's Bay coats, parkas, Inuit crafts and carvings, knitted goods, and snow boots and moccasins.

Waterloo

The Waterloo area has a wide variety of things to offer visitors. The **Laurel Creek Nature Centre** is located on woodlots that are rich with vegetation and wildlife. More than 160 plant species have been identified in the nature centre as well as over 105 species of birds. There's a floating observation platform in the marsh with a bird-watching blind along it. Nature trails wind their way through the area also. The actual Nature Centre Building includes a visitor centre and two classrooms. Programs are offered there for community groups, schools, and families, and can be arranged by phoning ahead. The Centre is located on Beaver Creek Road, northwest of Waterloo.

There's also some fine vegetation on display at the **Waterloo Farmer's Market.** The market features meat and crafts as well as produce. It's located just off Highway 85 at Weber St. and it's open Saturdays, Mondays, and Wednesdays from June to October.

There's an unusual museum in Waterloo that would be of special interest to those interested in games. **The Museum and Archives of Games** at 415 Philip St. shows the history and development of games played around the world. It's open afternoons from Monday to Friday.

There's also an antique dealer you might enjoy paying a visit to in Waterloo. **Duke's Antiques** at 16 William St. E. features china, glass, metals, and furniture.

Children always enjoy seeing animals, so if you're looking for somewhere to take them, consider the **Waterloo Park and Zoo.** This complex features a wide variety of native animals including wolves, bears, and birds. It also has two swimming pools, a lake, and a potter's workshop. It's situated on Albert St.

There are several country dining places found in small towns not far from Waterloo. **Angie's Kitchen** in

Fried fruit fantasy

Apple fritters are a delicious Pennsylvania-Dutch tradition. You'll find them at maple syrup festivals, and other Waterloo County fairs. You can easily make them at home — choose from the traditional sliced apple approach, or chop the apples. Either way, they make a great dessert or snack.

Apple Fritters

Core, peel, and slice or chop 2 or 3 apples (Macs make great fritters). Mix 1 beaten egg and 1 cup milk, into 1 cup flour, 1 teaspoon baking powder and 2 tablespoons sugar. It should be a fairly thick batter. Dip and coat each slice, or mix in the chopped apples. Drop into hot fat (240 C), and cook, turning once, until golden brown. Drain on paper towels and either dip into a sugar and cinnamon mixture (try this method for easy coating: place sugar, cinnamon and a fritter in a brown paper bag, close and shake), or serve with maple syrup.

St. Agatha is housed in a hotel that was built in 1839. This restaurant features early Canadian decor and home style cooking, including bread and pastries baked on the premises. It's located at 85 Erb St. W. Southwest of Waterloo in New Hamburg, is a fine French restaurant called **The Waterlot.** It's situated at 17 Huron St. in a Victorian house with several elegant dining rooms. The **Blue Moon Hotel,** west of Waterloo, serves Pennsylvania Dutch and German cuisine. It's housed in a home built in 1855. The dining room is decorated with Mennonite artifacts.

Welland

Welland is best known for its steel products, canal, and roses. And the **Welland Historical Museum** contains artifacts and photographs that illustrate the founding and history of the city as well as describe its position as a trade and transportation centre today. The museum is located in the Solomon Moore House at 656 South Pelham St. and is open afternoons from Victoria Day weekend until Thanksgiving. It is closed on Mondays. If you happen to visit Welland on a weekend, you might enjoy a visit to its **Flea Market.** It's held at the Niagara Regional Exhibition Centre every Sunday.

Wiarton

One of the most popular activities in the Wiarton area is fishing, and you're not likely to see more fish in any one place than you will at the **Fish Hatchery.** There you'll see both live fish and displays relating to fish. It's located 2 km north of town on the lakeshore. The Hatchery is open year round, but it's limited to displays rather than live fish from July to October.

Twelve miles north of Wiarton you can visit the **Cape Croker Indian Reserve.** This is a large Ojibway community with a reconstructed Indian fort, craft shops, and picnic areas. The Reserve is open to visitors year round.

Just south of Wiarton is a store you might enjoy called **Summer Kitchen Antiques.** Its specialties include early Canadian furniture, Victorian furniture, old stoves, ironware, pottery, and pressed glass.

Windsor

There are some good country things to do in the Windsor area. One of the most interesting activities would be a trip to the **Ojibway Park Nature Study Centre.** Exhibits at the centre focus on wilderness concerns such as forest ecology, wildlife conservation, and fire as a park-management tool. Groups visiting the site can arrange to hear a naturalist speak on an ecological theme or have him or her conduct a nature hike in the park. Literature and audio-visual aids are also available for teachers and group leaders.

Another country thing to do in Windsor is to visit **The Farm.** Children will enjoy this park designed for them in a rural setting. Attractions include farm animals, rides, and animated characters. The Farm is situated at 9009 Howard Avenue and is open daily from May to October.

There's a real farm near Windsor

that might be of more interest to adults. **Walker Orchards** is a farm produce outlet that specializes in apples, peaches, corn, tomatoes, and potatoes. It's located north of the Windsor Airport on E.C. Rowe between Walker and Pellete Rds.

Towns Index

125

Towns Index

Town	Area Map	Town	Area Map	Town	Area Map	Town	Area Map
Green Valley	7	Kingsville	1	McKellar	5	Orillia	5
Grimsby	4	Kinmount	5	Meaford	3	Oro	5
Guelph	2	Kirkfield	5	Melbourne	1	Orono	4
		Kirkland Lake	8	Merrickville	7	Oshawa	4
Haliburton	6	Kirkton	1	Metcalfe	7	Ottawa	7
Hall's Lake	5	Kitchener	2	Middleville	6	Owen Sound	3
Hamilton	4	Kleinburg	4	Midhurst	5		
Hanover	3	Komoka	1	Midland	5	Pakenham	7
Harcourt	6			Mildmay	3	Paisley	3
Harriston	3	Lakefield	6	Millbrook	6	Palmerston	3
Harrow	1	Langton	2	Milton	4	Parham	6
Harrowsmith	6	Lansdowne	7	Milverton	2	Paris	2
Hearst	8	Leamington	1	Minden	5	Parkhill	1
Heidleberg	2	Lindsay	4	Mitchell	2	Parry Sound	5
Hensall	1	Linwood	2	Morrisburg	7	Pembroke	7a
Highgate	1	Listowel	3	Mount Forest	3	Penetanguishene	5
Hillsburg	4	Lombardy	7	Murillo	8	Petawa	7a
Huntsville	5	London	2			Perth	7
Huttonville	4	Lucan	1	Napanee	6	Peterborough	6
Hymers	8	Lucknow	3	Navan	7	Petrolia	1
				Neustadt	3	Picton	6
Ilderton	1	Maberly	6	New Hamburg	2	Point Alexander	7a
Ingersoll	2	Madoc	6	Newington	7	Poplar Hill	1
Iron Bridge	3a	Magnetawan	5	New Liskeard	8	Porquis Junction	8
Iroquois	7	Manitouwadge	8	Niagara Falls	4	Pt. Burwell	2
Iroquois Falls	8	Manitoulin Island	3a	Niagara-on-the-Lake	4	Port Colborne	4
		Manitowaning	3a	Nipigon	8	Port Dover	2
Jarvis	4	Maple	4	North Bay	5	Port Elgin	3
Jordan	4	Markdale	3	Norwich	2	Port Hope	6
		Markham	4	Norwood	6	Port Perry	4
Kapuskasing	8	Marmora	6			Port Rowan	2
Keene	6	Massey	3a			Port Stanley	2
Keewatin	8	Matheson	8	Oakville	4	Port Sydney	5
Kemptville	7	Mattawa	5	Oakwood	4	Powassan	5
Kenora	8	Maynooth	6	Odessa	6	Prescott	7
Kincardine	3	Maxville	7	Oil Springs	1	Preston	2
Kingston	6	McDonald's Corners	6	Orangeville	3	Providence Bay	3a

126

Towns Index

	Area Map		Area Map		Area Map		Area Map
Ravenswood	1	Stoney Creek	4	Varna	1	Westmeath	7a
Renfrew	7a	Stoney Point	1	Vermilion Bay	8	Wheatley	1
Riceville	7	Stouffville	4	Vineland	4	Whitby	4
Richard's Landing	8	Stratford	2			Wiarton	3
Richmond Hill	4	Strathroy	1	Wainfleet	4	Wilberforce	6
Ridgetown	1	Streetsville	4	Walkerton	3	Williamstown	7
Ripley	3	Sudbury	8	Warsaw	6	Windsor	1
Rocklyn	3	Sunderland	4	Waterloo	2	Wingham	3
Rockton	4	Sundridge	5	Watford	1	Winona	4
Rodney	1	Sweaburg	2	Wasaga Beach	5	Woodbridge	4
Roseneath	6	Syndenham	6	Wawa	8	Woodstock	2
Rosseau	5			Welland	4	Wyoming	1
Russell	7	Tara	3	Wellesley	2		
		Tavistock	2	West Lorne	1	Zurich	1
St. Catharines	4	Tecumseh	1				
St. Jacob's	2	Teeswater	3				
St. Mary's	2	Teeterville	2				
St. Thomas	2	Temagami	8				
Saltford	3	Terra Cotta	4				
Sarnia	1	Thamesville	1				
Sault Ste. Marie	8	Thedford	1				
Schomberg	4	Thornbury	3				
Seaforth	2	Thorndale	2				
Severn Bridge	5	Thunder Bay	8				
Shannonville	6	Tilbury	1				
Shedden	2	Tillsonburg	2				
Shelburne	3	Timmins	8				
Simcoe	2	Tiverton	3				
Sioux Narrows	8	Toronto	4				
Smiths Falls	7	Trenton	6				
Smithville	4	Trout Creek	5				
Snowball	4	Tweed	6				
South Mountain	7						
South River	5	Uxbridge	4				
Spencerville	7						
Stirling	6	Vanleek Hill	7				

**Province of Ontario
Travel Information Centres**

Barrie (705) 726-0932
Cornwall (613) 933-2420
Fort Frances (807) 274-3259
Niagara Falls (416) 358-3761
Ottawa (613) 237-6280
Sarnia (519) 344-7403
Sault Ste. Marie (705) 253-8572
Toronto (416) 965-4008
Windsor (519) 252-8368

Ontario

Guide to area maps

Map 8

Map 5

Map 7

Map 6

Map 3

Map 4

Map 2

Map
1

Area Map 1

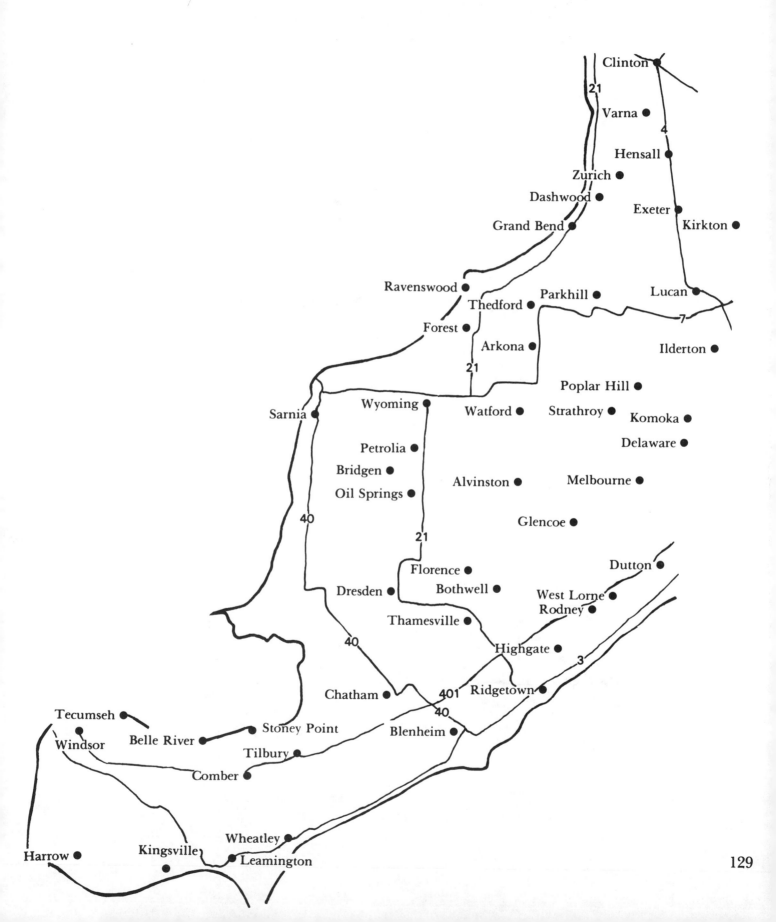

Area Map 2

Area Map 3

Iron Bridge
Blind River
Massey
68

Manitoulin Island
68
Manitowaning
Providence Bay

6
Wiarton

Owen Sound
21

Meaford
Thornbury

Collingwood

Tara
Chatsworth
Rocklyn

Desboro

Port Elgin

21

Paisley
Chesley

Tiverton

Markdale
Feversham

Flesherton
4

24

Kincardine

6

Hanover
Durham
Dundalk

Walkerton
9

Ripley
Neustadt
Mildmay
Ayton
10

86
Teeswater
Shelburne

Lucknow
Belmore
Mount Forest

Wingham
Harriston
Orangeville

Dungannon
Gorrie
Grand Valley

Bluevale
9

Saltford
4
Palmerston
Arthur

Blyth
86
Listowel
6

Goderich
Brussels
Drayton

8

131

Area Map 4

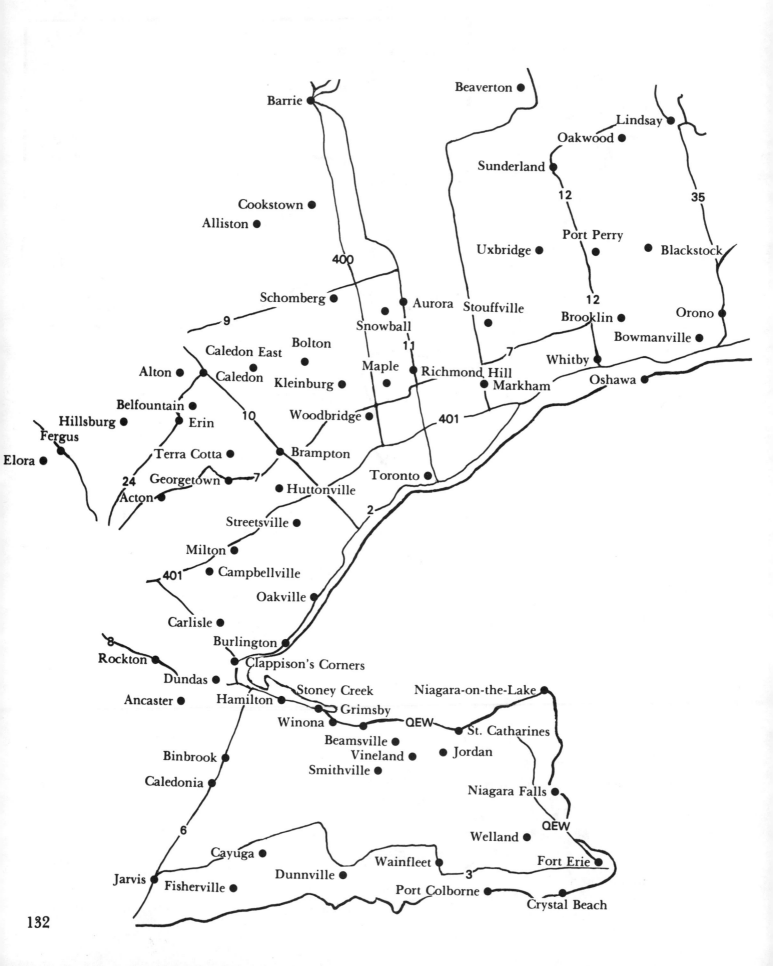

Area Map 5

North Bay

Mattawa

Callander

Bonfield ●

17

Powassan

Trout Creek

South River

Sundridge

Magnetawan ●

Dunchurch ●

Burk's Falls

69

Bayfield ●

Emsdale

60

McKellar ●

11

69

Parry Sound ●

Huntsville

Rosseau ●

Dorset ●

Port Sydney ●

35

Hall's Lake ●

Bracebridge ●

Bala ●

69

Minden ●

Gravenhurst ●

Penetanguishene ●

Severn Bridge

Kinmount ●

Midland ●

Coldwater ●

27

121

Elmvale ●

Orillia ●

35

Wasaga Beach ●

Bobcaygeon ●

27

11

Kirkfield ●

Fenelon Falls ●

133

Midhurst ●

36

Area Map 6

Algonquin Park

60

60

Barry's Bay

Eganville

41

Calabogie

Maynooth

Harcourt

Bancroft

Denbigh

Middleville

121

Wilberforce

McDonald's Corners

Haliburton

41

Gooderham

Coe Hill

Maberly

Apsley

Cloyne

7

36

Parham

Lakefield

Warsaw

Marmora

Madoc

Tweed

41

Norwood

7

Centreville

Sydenham

62

Harrowsmith

Peterborough

Campbellford

Stirling

Keene

401

Napanee

Odessa

Kingston

Roseneath

62

Shannonville

Millbrook

Belleville

Bewdley

Brighton

401

Trenton

Picton

Cobourg

Bloomfield

Port Hope

134

Area Map 7

Point Alexander

17

Petawa
Pembroke
Westmeath
41
Beachburg

17
Renfrew

Arnprior
Pakenham
17
Carp
Almonte

Ottawa
Clarence Creek
Navan
Riceville
Vanleek Hill

34

Maxville
Alexandria

16
Russell
Metcalfe

Green Valley

Avonmore
Williamstown

7
Chesterville
Newington

Kemptville
South Mountain

401
Cornwall

Perth
Smiths Falls
Merrickville
Morrisburg

Lombardy 29
Spencerville
Iroquois

15

Prescott

Delta
Brockville

15

Lansdowne 401

Gananoque

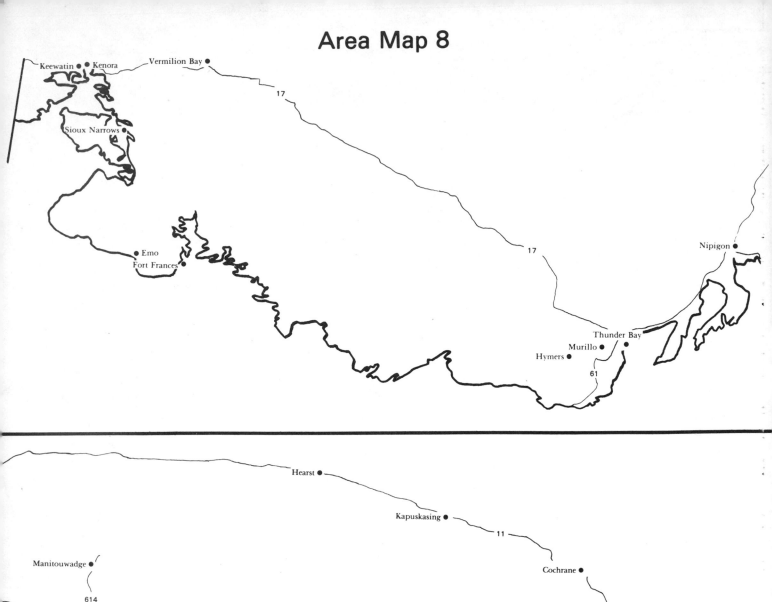

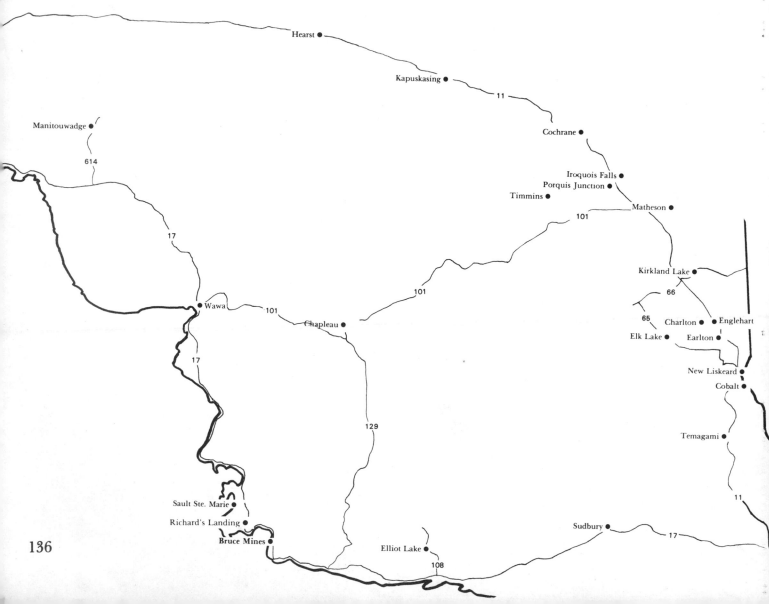